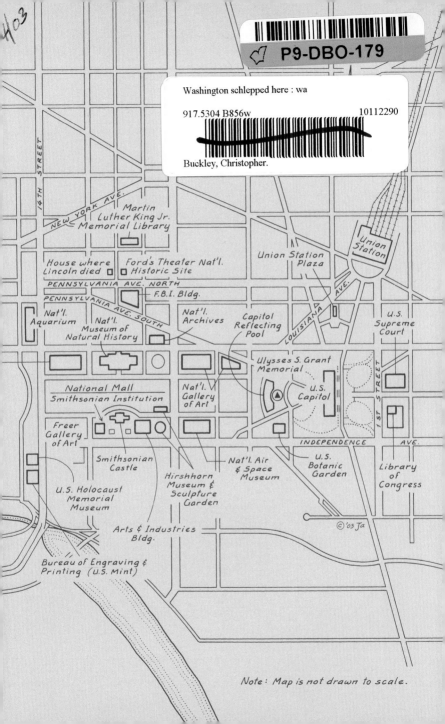

14TH STREET

NEW YORK AVE.

Martin Luther King Jr. Memorial Library

House where Lincoln died

Ford's Theater Nat'l. Historic Site

Union Station Plaza

Union Station

PENNSYLVANIA AVE. NORTH

PENNSYLVANIA AVE. SOUTH

F.B.I. Bldg.

Nat'l. Aquarium

Nat'l. Museum of Natural History

Nat'l. Archives

Capitol Reflecting Pool

LOUISIANA AVE.

U.S. Supreme Court

Ulysses S. Grant Memorial

U.S. Capitol

1 ST STREET

National Mall
Smithsonian Institution

Nat'l. Gallery of Art

Freer Gallery of Art

Smithsonian Castle

Hirshhorn Museum & Sculpture Garden

Nat'l. Air & Space Museum

INDEPENDENCE AVE.

U.S. Botanic Garden

Library of Congress

U.S. Holocaust Memorial Museum

Arts & Industries Bldg.

© '03 Ja

Bureau of Engraving & Printing (U.S. Mint)

Note: Map is not drawn to scale.

Washington Schlepped Here

ALSO IN THE CROWN JOURNEYS SERIES

Washington Schlepped Here

WALKING IN THE NATION'S CAPITAL

Christopher Buckley

CROWN JOURNEYS

CROWN PUBLISHERS · NEW YORK

Title page photograph © Joseph Sohm; Visions of America / CORBIS

Copyright © 2003 by Christopher Buckley

Published by Crown Journeys, an imprint of Crown Publishers, New York. Member of the Crown Publishing Group, a division of Random House, Inc. www.randomhouse.com

Crown Journeys and the Crown Journeys colophon are trademarks of Random House, Inc.

Printed in the United States of America

Design by Lauren Dong
Map by Jackie Aher

Library of Congress Cataloging-in-Publication Data
Buckley, Christopher, 1952–
    Washington schlepped here : walking in the nation's capital /
    Christopher Buckley.— 1st ed.
    1. Washington Region—Tours. 2. Washington (D.C.)—Tours.
3. Walking—Washington Region—Guidebooks. 4. Walking—
Washington (D.C.)—Guidebooks. I. Title. II. Series.
    F192.3 .B83 2003
    917.5304'42—dc21   2002151365

ISBN 1-4000-4687-4

First Edition

For Conor,
First-generation Washingtonian

By Way of Explanation . . .

WHEN CROWN—an ironic name, it only now occurs to me, for the publisher of a book about Washington, D.C.—asked me to write a walking tour book about the city, I replied, "Sure, but can I drive?" It's a big town and it can get awfully warm. "No way," they replied. The editor also said—a bit rudely, to my way of thinking—"You look as though you could use a walk." True enough, at 355 pounds, I had perhaps "let myself go." So after consulting with my family and various medical authorities, I proposed, "Okay, but you pay half the funeral expenses if I drop dead on the steps of the Lincoln Memorial." I also demanded burial at Arlington National Cemetery. After prolonged negotiations with the authorities, it turns out that you cannot be buried there if you were deemed medically unfit and never served a day in the U.S. Armed Forces. It is my hope that this colossal injustice will someday be rectified. At any rate, I didn't die, and am thrilled to report that I am now down to a svelte 340 pounds, and that everywhere I go, I hear those delightful words, "You've lost weight!" To be paid to shed pounds while exploring a city that I love—well, now I can truly say, "Is this a great country, or what?"

I came here in July 1981. Like many others who came here to Washington to work for the government, I was certain it would be temporary. It is now July 2002, and here I still am.

The late Joseph W. Alsop (another Connecticut transplant) once wrote that no matter how long one lives here—and he did, conspicuously, for over half a century—it somehow never *feels* permanent. He called himself, "that sad and rootless thing: a 'Washingtonian.'" Cave Dwellers, that is, Washingtonians whose families have lived here since the Pleistocene epoch and generally make sure you're aware of it, would probably sniff at that, but then they sniff at pretty much everything.

The day I moved here, I got lost driving down and ended up on New York Avenue. It was a warm summer night and I had the top down on my Volkswagen Rabbit, and I had no idea where I was, when suddenly I looked up and there was the gleaming white dome of the U.S. Capitol. It was like a scene in a movie, and I still get a lump in my throat every time I think about that moment. I suspect almost everyone who comes here to work for the government harbors, deep down, a Jimmy Stewart–*Mr. Smith Goes to Washington* fantasy. A few minutes later I was driving past the White House, and the Old Executive Office

Building next to it, where I would report to work the next day. I thought, *What an adventure this is going to be.*

Next morning I presented myself to the Secret Service guard at the White House southwest gate, drenched in sweat after the five-block walk from my Foggy Bottom rental, only to be told that my name wasn't in the computer so they weren't going to let me in. Washington is very good at bringing youthful dreamers back to earth.

They let me in eventually, and I did have adventures. I worked at the White House for two years, married a beautiful CIA officer, who still refuses to tell me what she did there. I wrote a novel called *The White House Mess* (the pun being that the staff dining room there is run by the navy and therefore called "The Mess").

Today the adventure is raising two children, and that's enough for any lifetime. But when I see those motorcades go by, I think back to the days when I used to ride in them (usually in the way, way back). When I look up and see *Marine Two* circling the U.S. Naval Observatory, preparing to pick up the vice president, I remember what the view looked like from up there. I remember being in the "War Room," in the bowels of the Pentagon. One time I had to act as a courier and carry top secret documents to the vice president. Another time, at an all-star baseball game, his military aide asked me to take care of the "Football," the briefcase containing the nuclear launch codes, while he went to the bathroom. Another time I got to press the launch trigger on a ballistic nuclear submarine and saw the instrument panel light up: MISSILE AWAY. I don't want to make too much of this nuclear thing, lest you begin to wonder about me, but at the time I was in my twenties and it seemed awfully sort of cool. They used to let me into the Situation Room at the White House whenever I knocked, and oh, the top secrets I heard! One night, exhausted and to be honest a little bit drunk after a grueling swing through Latin America that had begun with the discovery of 75 pounds of plastic explosives under the threshold of our runway in Bogotá, the vice president's press secretary and I hijacked *Air Force Two* on the way back from Rio. (We wanted a night's R&R in Rio— Mr. Bush wanted to return to Washington so he could play tennis. Revolutions have started over less.) The vice president effectively quashed our uprising by turning down the volume on the plane's loudspeaker as I read our demands. I have a photo of it. At the bottom, he wrote that I was forgiven, but that my punishment was to write 16 speeches a week, "all on the theme 'respect for the office.'" George Bush—this would be George H.W. Bush—was and is as fine and decent and lovely man as I have ever known, and it was a privilege and honor to work my young butt off for him.

It will quickly become apparent that I'm no historian. Moreover, that I know nothing about architecture, art, politics, and for that matter, landscaping. This begs the question: *So why are you writing this book?* The answer: I may not be a historian and that other stuff, but I know how to steal from historians. And not only have I stolen from historians but I also have stolen from some of the guides—such as Anthony Pitch, whose walking tours I took as part of the research for this book. These wise docents of the sidewalks are the true lovers of the city, passionate about its history and generous in their telling of it, and if you're not too exhausted by the time we finish you really should sign up for their tours.

A brief word about the title before we put on comfy shoes and get started. It's not bad, I think. I say this not to boast, but by way of pointing out that I never could have come up with it myself. Crown pestered me for a title—in fact, they were a downright nuisance—months and months before the book was due. To get rid of them, I suggested *Das Capital.* Clever, *ja?* Well, they loved it. But then it dawned on me that no one would buy a book about Washington, D.C., with that title, except maybe for one or two pointy-heads of twisted sensibility from a think tank looking for a cheap present to give a nephew they didn't much like. Crown generously gave me 15 minutes to come up with a new one, or *Das Capital* it was going to be. I was bemoaning my predicament to my *Forbes FYI* magazine colleague Patrick Cooke, and just like that he said, "Washington Schlepped Here." So if you need a title, call Patrick.

Otherwise I was going to call it *Jackie's Washington,* for the reason that when I showed up for Mary Kay Ricks's Jackie Kennedy's Georgetown walking tour, it looked like the Million Mom March. I was nearly trampled to death. As I write, the Corcoran Gallery has a Jackie Kennedy exhibit. The line for it starts in Alexandria, Virginia. Put "Jackie's" in front of anything, and they will come. I must try this with my next book, whatever it's about. Meanwhile, I hope you'll enjoy "Buckley's" Washington, even if it's a poor substitute. If I have nothing to offer by way of scholarship, I do love the place and plan to stay here even if those dunderheads at Arlington refuse to bury me with full military honors. Maybe I'll have my executors sneak in at night and scatter my ashes next to Pierre Charles L'Enfant's grave, which has absolutely the best view in town.

A Pretty Brief History of
Why They Put It Here

I'M WRITING THIS in July. The temperature is in the midnineties, with humidity in the Brazilian rain forest level, and the radio is broadcasting one of those warnings telling you for God's sake, don't let your children outside. So it seems logical, even a good thing, as Martha Stewart used to say, to pose the question: Why did they decide to put it here, instead of, say, Lake Champlain, or for that matter, Montréal? Surely it would have been worth a quick war with the French, even if they did help us win the Revolution.

The answer, sadly, is typical Washington bureaucratic shortsightedness. There is no evidence that it ever even occurred to the Founding Fathers or to the Continental Congress to put the new capital where the climate was perfect and where they already had lots of excellent French restaurants. Instead, they settled on a swampy bank of the Potomac (pronounced Po-to-mac) River, just downstream from a tobacco port named Georgetown (pronounced George-town).

Between 1774 and 1789, the Continental Congress met in Philadelphia, Baltimore, Philadelphia, Lancaster, York, Philadelphia, Princeton, Annapolis, Trenton, and New York City. One wit of the time suggested it would be easier to put the Congress on wheels and roll it from place to place. Abusing the Congress has been an American pastime from the beginning.

In June of 1783, while the Congress was in session in Philadelphia's Independence Hall, debating a bill requiring air bags and rear brake lights on stagecoaches, 300 soldiers did something soldiers are not technically supposed to do—they surrounded Independence Hall and pointed their muskets at the windows and used offensive language. This was not a drill. They had not been paid. When you don't pay the army, problems generally result. This is why today, the U.S. government from time to time secretly steps in and meets the payroll of the Russian navy. Disgruntled postal workers shooting up the office is one thing; disgruntled Russkies with submarine-launched nukes is another.

At any rate, there being no metal detectors or Jersey barriers or tear gas back in 1783, the Congress immediately attached a rider to the Air Bags bill authorizing an immediate move to Princeton. The bill sailed through the Subcommittee on Highway Safety and became law. General Washington, meanwhile, unamused by this display of testosterone, hanged two of the soldiers and had another four flogged for good measure.

Princeton cannot have been thrilled by becoming Host City to a bunch of grubby politicians, especially since they demanded to be admitted to its elite eating clubs. The homelessness of the Congress had, finally, reached a critical point. Something had to be done.

Two locations for a permanent seat of government were proposed, one near Trenton, another near Georgetown, Maryland. Oddly, northern congressmen favored the former, whereas southerners favored the latter. This caused intense bickering and very nearly led to the dissolution of the fledgling United States. Congressional leaders, however, prevailed on the representatives to "postpone Civil War until 1861 or thereabouts, when we shall doubtless have a more efficient means of slaughtering each other." (That's not an exact quote, but I'm sure someone said it.)

Seven years of bitter debate followed. John Adams of Massachusetts wanted to put it in Germantown, Pennsylvania. It is fortunate that Adams was overruled, for this would have caused tragic miscommunications centuries later during World War II, with military dispatches being sent to the wrong capital.

Finally, one evening in 1790, over a dinner of "savory viands and mellow Madeira," Alexander Hamilton of New York and Thomas Jefferson of Virginia worked out a compromise: Jefferson would let Hamilton have sex with his slaves if Hamilton would let Jefferson cheat at bezique.

Additionally, the North would consent to placing this new "Federal City" on the Potomac if the South in turn would agree to pay its share of the bill for the Revolutionary War. The so-called Residence Bill was approved on July 16, 1790, amid murmuring from the northern delegation that the new site would prove to be "hotter than the inside of a Microwave Oven." These would prove to be prophetic words indeed, but at least the matter was settled. It seems fitting that a city that usually goes for the compromise should have begun with one.

After schlepping up and down the Potomac (still pronounced Po-to-mac) by January 1791, President Washington had made up his mind where exactly to put the new Federal City, as it was then called: on about 10 square miles (roughly the size, at the time, of London) between Rock Creek and the Eastern Branch of the Potomac (now the Anacostia River). Washington knew the area well. In 1755 he had crossed the Potomac going north with General Edward Braddock to fight the French and Indians. They crossed about where the Theodore Roosevelt Memorial Bridge now is. Braddock was later killed in a fierce and sanguinary ambush at the forks of the Ohio, during which his young aide Lt. Col. Washington had two horses shot out from under him. The remnant of the rock where he and Washington landed on the eastern bank of the Potomac is still there—underneath a manhole at the bottom of a well by the approach to the Theodore Roosevelt Memorial Bridge near the Kennedy Center.

Unless you're a really die-hard Braddock fan, it might suffice just to know it's there.

By sheer coincidence, the new capital that Washington selected was within easy commuting distance of his estate in Mount Vernon, 16 miles away. He immediately instructed Congress to pass a bill widening the bridle path to Mount Vernon to four lanes, with toll booths every three miles, clearly marked exit ramps, a High Occupancy Carriage lane for rush hour, with all concession rights controlled by his wife, Martha. Congress defiantly refused the concession rights, grumbling that "we did not defeat one tyrant named George only to replace him with another." Washington received the unwelcome news while he was sitting for the famous portrait by Gilbert Stuart, a fact that historians suggest accounts for the president's pinched expression.

There remained only one task: actually building the new capital city. There was a saying at the time: "If you want to design a new capital, hire a Frenchman."

Major Pierre Charles L'Enfant was at the time a 35-year-old military engineer who had volunteered to fight with the Americans in the Continental Army, at his own expense. His father had been "Painter in ordinary to the King." Pierre in turn became "artist extraordinary" to the army, proving that even then, America was already a great country. He executed likenesses of General Washington, including one done at Valley Forge. Drawing heroic portraits of the boss during a horrible winter is probably a smart way to get yourself into his good graces. He also decorated ballrooms and built banquet halls. At any rate, by 1791, the by now 37-year-old L'Enfant was on the scene, raring to go: an artist, engineer, and city planner who had grown up in the world's most beautiful capital city, Paris, amid spectacular buildings and palaces and gardens and boulevards, the Louvre, Champs Élysées, *le works.*

Two years earlier, he had petitioned Washington to say that he wanted to design "the Capital of this vast Empire." America being more or less bankrupt and war-ravaged, it was debatable just how "vast" this notional "Empire" was ever going to be. But then the French have always been uncannily prescient about America (see *le tout* de Tocqueville).

L'Enfant told Washington, ". . . it will be obvious that the plan should be drawn on such a scale as to leave room for that aggrandizement and embellishment which the increase of the wealth of the Nation will permit it to pursue to any period, however remote." In other words, think big, and it will come. It's an architectural sentiment that would be echoed over a century later by the designer of Union Station, whose motto was, "Make no little plans. They have no magic to stir men's blood. . . ."

L'Enfant's plan, worked out in consultation with Thomas Jefferson and Washington, resembled a neat geometric spiderweb, with 160-foot-wide avenues intersecting circles and squares. Streets radiated out from the circles and squares in threes, a Renaissance notion called a *patte d'oie,* or goose's foot, that permitted three simultaneous vistas from a single viewpoint, a sort of visual *ménage à trois.* One avenue was actually 400 feet across and a mile long. Today we know it as the Mall.

There were three focal points: a capitol building atop a hill that he described as "a pedestal waiting for a monument," the "President's Palace" that in the fullness of time would become known as *le White House,* and an "Equestrian Figure" of Washington. This latter object was never built, owing to Washington's aversion to grandiosity. He didn't even want the city named after him, but that was a nonstarter. Instead, nearly a century later after an embarrassing hiatus, a 555-foot-high obelisk was finally completed, 300 feet southeast of the site L'Enfant had originally designated, sparing the Father of Our Country the perpetual indignity of the Conqueror Pigeon.

A grand plan it was, indeed, a masterpiece—the first truly capital city planned from scratch. Washington struck a deal with the landowners and appointed commissioners to oversee L'Enfant's work. At this point, either L'Enfant's Gallic or artistic temperament (or both) created fault lines up and down the city. He did not get along with the commissioners, ignoring their protests about the avenues and questions of eminent domain, refusing even a request for a copy of his plan and telling them to go jump in *le* Potomac. Washington ended up having to mediate the disputes, caught between indignant commissioners and landowners and his hothouse orchid city planner. But he recognized L'Enfant's genius and, in a letter to the commissioners, fretted lest "he should take miff and leave the business." The penultimate disaster came when L'Enfant personally began knocking down the house of Mr. Daniel Carroll of Duddington, original owner of the hill upon which the new capitol was to perch. Mr. Carroll was less than amused. President Washington wrote to the commissioners, "I receive with real mortification the account of the demolition of Mr. Carroll's house, by Major L'Enfant . . . against his consent." The final calamity was L'Enfant's demand that the commissioners be sacked and refusing to provide engraved plans for the advertised sale of lots.

Washington wrote L'Enfant a pained letter imploring him to get with the program. But he soon concluded that whatever L'Enfant's talents were, harmonious relations with the client were not among them. L'Enfant was dismissed. He was offered one or two few golden parachutes, but out of pride, spurned them all and, eerily prefiguring one aspect of the American temperament, spent the rest of his life suing the government. He died in abject poverty near Bladensburg, Maryland, where people of the era used to go in order to kill each other in duels. We shall pay proper *hommage* to poor L'Enfant when we visit Arlington National Cemetery, where in 1909 he was finally moved from his pauper's grave and reburied with full honors.

Meanwhile, *allons-nous* and begin our *promenades* in the city that he left us.

Walk One

Union Station

To board a train in New York's Penn Station is to descend into Dante's *Inferno*. To disembark in Washington's Union Station is to ascend into his *Paradiso*. This is one of the world's truly spectacular thresholds, and you're lucky, because for the first seven years I lived in Washington, it was shut for renovations—after the Congress, in its infinite wisdom, spent many millions turning it into a—it makes me twitch even to type the words—National Visitors Center for the Bicentennial in 1976. Only the United States Congress could have taken one of the country's most stunning interior spaces and turned it into, as E. J. Applewhite noted in his excellent book, *Washington Itself,* "a labyrinth of makeshift passages and a mean borax lobby that would disgrace a small-town motel . . . an unseemly pit with escalators to nowhere but with a large screen for an automated slide show called

PAVE (for Primary Audio Visual Experience) to orient the visitor to sights he can see better by simply walking out to the sidewalk in front of the building."

I feel much better for having quoted that. To paraphrase Santayana, those who forget how Congress can waste your money are doomed to supply it with even more. But let us relax now into the beauty of this cathedral of transportation, while trying to forget for the moment that Congress is now in charge of "reforming" Amtrak.

It makes sense to start our first walk here, for two reasons. The first and obvious one is that this might well be where you're arriving. The second is that Union Station was built at the turn of the century as part of a plan to finish what L'Enfant had begun. The station's architect was a man named Daniel H. Burnham, a Chicagoan who had been director of works for the Chicago Columbian Exposition of 1893. The Exposition's "Court of Honor," displaying buildings of even height, with lots and lots of statues and fountains, got America's architects to thinking that the slightly shabby, thrown-together *mélange* that was the nation's capital could use some brightening up.

This led to the McMillan Commission of 1901, headed by Senator James McMillan of Michigan, a railroad magnate. And now I must eat my words about how Congress screws up everything, because in this case, it didn't. What it did was to appoint the country's aesthetic A-Team—Burnham; New York architect Charles F. McKim; landscape architect Frederick Law Olmsted, Jr.; and sculptor Augustus Saint-Gaudens—and send them on a seven-week tour of Europe to gather up ideas, then turn them loose on the capital city. The result, a Rome-on-the-Potomac landscape of gleaming white granite and marble buildings squatting on a vast green lawn, is the city that you are now standing in. Its trophies are Union Station, the Lincoln Memorial, the Reflecting Pool, the Memorial Bridge to Arlington, the Federal Triangle. L'Enfant's Renaissance city, reborn as a Beaux Arts showcase.

Union Station's vast scale isn't simply due to the fact that its builder tended to think big, but has a more practical reason: to accommodate the crowds at presidential inaugurals. As Applewhite notes, every president from Woodrow Wilson to Harry Truman arrived here by train for his inauguration. When the hotels reached maximum occupancy, visitors slept in Pullman sleeping cars on sidings. FDR's and Eisenhower's funeral trains set out from here. Robert F. Kennedy's arrived here. These were great events that took place on a worthy stage. The spectacle of coffins loaded onto military planes in air force hangars or tarmacs have little of the same grandeur.

The building that Union Station replaced was the old Baltimore and Ohio Railroad Station. It was here that Abraham Lincoln, under conditions of secrecy and disguise, arrived for his inaugural in 1861, and from here that the funeral train carrying his martyred remains departed for the long journey home in 1865. The trip to Washington, fraught with peril and threat of assassination as it was, had its comic moments, not that they were funny at the time. Lincoln's young son Robert managed to lose his father's inaugural speech, and once Lincoln had been successfully sneaked into the ladies' entrance to Willard's Hotel, his bodyguard Allan Pinkerton cabled in code to his fellow agents: "Plums delivered nuts safely!" Presidential guards are no longer allowed to send cables.

Burnham based the Union Station's central hall on the one in the Baths of Diocletian in Rome. I just looked up Diocletian in the encyclopedia: aside from imposing wage and price controls throughout the Roman Empire—making him the Richard Nixon of his day—his other distinction seems to be that he conducted the last great persecution of Christians. Whatever his sins, by Jupiter, he made sure Romans bathed.

There is a definite "Roman thing"—as my former boss, Vice President Bush, would have put it—going on in Washington. To be sure, Gore Vidal has written more or less his entire impressive *oeuvre* on this theme. At the city's beginning, there was even a creek named "Tiber" running where Constitution Avenue now does. Rome had Marcello Mastroianni and Anita Ekberg splashing in the Trevi fountain; we got Wilbur Mills and Fanne Foxe leaping into the Tidal Basin. But Washington may be the only modern city left with functioning Roman-style temples. By functioning, I don't mean that people are slitting open peacocks and roasting bullocks. The Park Service would probably fine you for that. But gods are being worshiped in these temples. We'll explore this more fully when we get to the Jefferson and Lincoln Memorials.

For now, set your bags down and enjoy the incredible space you're in. Then walk to the main doors, where you'll hear Jimmy Stewart bubbling over with excitement: "Oh, look, look! There it is! The Capitol Dome!"

United States Capitol

The Zero Milestone, a little nub of stone marking the precise spot from which all distances from Washington are supposed to be measured, is just south of the White House. The Capitol Building, meanwhile, is the Zero Milestone of American democracy. Any movie set in Washington, any *New Yorker* cartoon, will show the dome perfectly framed in a window. It is the ur-symbol for "United States of America." To be sure, there are days—most days, perhaps—when what goes on inside this gleaming white hive is enough to make you wonder if we really did the right thing back in 1776.

There's a wonderful oil painting from 1844 done by William McLeod showing what Capitol Hill looked like from where Union Station is today. It could be a tranquil Constable landscape depicting Wiltshire or the Cotswolds, only there's this odd Roman temple plunked down in the middle of it.

The landscape that greets you today as you walk out of the Union Station is slightly changed. The first thing you'll probably notice is the absence of cows. But once you've crossed Massachusetts Avenue, and you start up the

Hill, it does get bucolic, if not quite by McLeod's standards. In 1809, according to the *WPA Guide,* the British ambassador "put up a covey of quail" right around here. *Et in Arcadia blam blam.*

In the 1870s, Jenkins Hill, the "pedestal" that L'Enfant had envisioned as "waiting for a monument" (the "Congress House"), was transformed into an urban garden space by landscape architect Frederick Law Olmsted. He had by then completed a masterpiece, New York's Central Park. Here he had 131 acres to sculpt, dig, and mulch. In the northwest corner of the grounds, just in from the intersection of First Street N.W. and Constitution Avenue, you'll find the grotto that he built over a spring once frequented by local Indian tribes and travelers on their way west, to Georgetown. It's apt that a bubbling spring should have later become a rendezvous point for Woodward and Bernstein and their famous source, "Deep Throat."

I stood somewhere near here on January 20, 1981, and watched Ronald Reagan become the 40th president. I remember being amazed to think that Reagan should become the first president in history to be sworn in on the West Front of the Capitol Building. Here this glorious expanse, the Mall, America's front lawn—why on *earth* had all those other presidents chosen to give their inaugural speeches facing—a parking lot? At any rate, Reagan the Californian decided to give his speech facing the same direction that Lewis and Clark had, and it seemed apt, even if on that particular day America was focused east, specifically in the direction of Iran, where our embassy hostages were still being held after 444 days. (Joke at the time: What's flat and glows in the dark? Tehran, ten minutes after Reagan is inaugurated.)

By standing on the West Front, Reagan was also facing Arlington National Cemetery. In his speech, he quoted from the diary of a young American soldier named Martin Treptow, who had been killed in World War I. Reagan said he would try to act as Treptow had pledged to "cheerfully and do my utmost, as if the issue of the whole struggle depended on me alone." It was a lovely sentiment, even if within a few hours the media had found out that that Martin Treptow wasn't buried at Arlington, but 1,100 miles away in Bloomer, Wisconsin. This would be the first of many clarifications over the next eight years issued by the White House press office. But I'll invoke my right as a Republican to go on remembering it as a stirring moment nonetheless, wherever the hell Marvin Treptow is buried. How many Republicans does it take to change a lightbulb? Three: one to change it, one to mix the martinis, one to reminisce about how good the old one was.

Let's continue on up the hill. Don't trip over any Jersey barriers. They're everywhere since 9/11. Tom Clancy wrote a book some years ago that ended with a vengeful Japanese flying a jumbo jet into the Capitol. How implausible!

The original plan was that L'Enfant would design the "Congress House" atop Jenkins Hill and see to its construction. But being L'Enfant, he crankily refused to provide any blueprints. When pressed, he grumped that it was all "in his head." Gone "to his head" might be more accurate. At any rate, once Washington sacked him, a design competition was announced, with $500 to go to the winner (about $8,900 today).

The winner was a Scottish doctor living in Tortola, British West Indies, who proudly announced, "I profess to have no knowledge of Architecture."

You're hired! This reminds me of *Mercury* astronaut Alan Shepard's quip about how reassuring it was, sitting there on top of a 78,000-pound Redstone rocket in the moments before blastoff, knowing that it had been "built by the lowest bidder."

Washington thought Dr. William Thornton's design beautiful and fitting, and Jefferson, who did know a thing or two about architecture, pronounced it "simple, noble, beautiful, excellently distributed, and moderate in size." To make up for his architectural shortcomings, Dr. Thornton "resolved to attempt this grand undertaking and study at the same time. I studied some months and worked almost night and day." You're always in good hands with a Scot.

On September 18, 1793, General Washington, wearing his Masonic apron embroidered by Madame Lafayette, laid and mortared the cornerstone. The occasion must have been impressive, but the image does make me smile. It doesn't help that in his remarks he declared the cornerstone "well and truly laid," but that's because I associate the phrase with Kingsley Amis's novels, in a rather different context. The fall of 1793 was momentous on both sides of the Atlantic: one month later, they chopped off Marie Antoinette's head in L'Enfant's hometown.

James Hoban, the Irish-born architect who was also working on the president's house just down the avenue, went to work. There were the usual difficulties with electricians and plumbers and bathroom tiles, but on November 17, 1800, the Congress of the United States convened in its new House. President John Adams addressed them the next day. His son, John Quincy Adams, who would serve as president and afterward as a nine-term congressman, died in the building forty-eight years later, after suffering a cerebral hemorrhage while giving a speech denouncing President Polk's Mexican War. (Good for you, Old Man Eloquent!) When you get to Statuary Hall, the original House of Representatives chamber, look for the plaque on the floor marking the spot where he fell. It's been too long since we lost a congressman this way.

The British paid the new building the compliment of trying to burn it to the ground on their swing through in August of 1814. The more you read about this appalling behavior, the more you wonder that the British ended up being our best friends. At any rate, their incendiary insults to our brand-new citadel of democracy required calling back architect Benjamin Latrobe, who had worked on the Capitol from 1802 to 1813, to restore what he called "a most magnificent ruin." He was succeeded in 1818 by Charles Bulfinch—"The First American Architect," according to my copy of *The City of Washington, An Illustrated*

History. By 1827, Bulfinch had erected the Capitol's first dome. Without detracting from his great achievement, this was not a dome you would confuse with say, the Pantheon or St. Peter's Basilica. To the eye accustomed to the present-day dome, it looked a bit like a half-full propane tank.

It wasn't until 1863, in the red-hot midst of the Civil War, that the dome we know was put up, under the direction of Thomas U. Walter of Philadelphia. It seems fitting that the capping of the Capitol should have been accomplished by a resident of the city in which the American Congress first met. Walter's supervising engineer was a man named Captain Montgomery C. Meigs, whom we will get to know better on our last walk.

It was no mean feat, installing this dome. Domes are tricky. It took Michelangelo to figure out how to put a dome on Saint Peter's. The Capitol's dome towers 288 feet above the eastern plaza and is 135 feet across at the base. It was made of cast iron, weighed 8.9 million pounds, and cost one million dollars. (About $14 million today.)

If you're putting up a really first-rate dome, you're going to need a radiator ornament. That statue that you can't quite see up there, but that you probably think, with reason, is an Indian in full feathered headdress, is actually Thomas Crawford's allegorical *Freedom*. It's 19 feet high and made of bronze, not that you really care. It was cast in the late 1850s, when Jefferson Davis, who would go on to become president of the Confederate States of America, was secretary of war. When he saw the liberty-type cap that Crawford had planned for *Freedom*'s head, Davis freaked out, thinking that it was subliminal advertising for the antislavery cause. Crawford substituted a crested helmet, which is why most people think that's a Native American up there, having the last laugh on the White Man. In 1993, *Freedom* was removed by helicopter for a much-needed de-crudding and waxing. It was quite a sight, watching her—him?—being lowered back into place. We all talked about it for days, but then we are a simple people, easily amused. At any rate, when we get to Arlington and delve more deeply into Montgomery C. Meigs, we'll have a chance to dwell on the irony of the fact that he and Jefferson Davis both played key roles in erecting the crown of American democracy.

Let's stand for a moment—if the Capitol Hill police will let us; they're awfully nervous these days—and look at the East Front, where all the presidents held their inaugurations. For the extra point, which two presidents were inaugurated neither here nor on the West Front? Good for you: William Howard Taft and Ronald Reagan—the second time, in 1985—who took their oaths and made their speeches inside the Great Rotunda owing to inclement weather. Reagan made the call when he was told that the seven-degree wind chill factor would cause the band's lips to stick to their instruments. To be honest, I'm a little disappointed we didn't get to watch that.

But the chill I'm feeling now, even on this warm spring day, is thinking about that famous photograph of the East Front showing Abraham Lincoln giving the most eloquent speech in American history, his second inaugural. Above and behind him you can make out the handsome face of John Wilkes Booth. Forty-one days later, he would get his chance for a clear shot. Sixty-nine days after Ronald Reagan was inaugurated on the other side of the building, he took a bullet fragment in his chest and very nearly died. Booth shot Lincoln to avenge the South; John Hinckley shot Reagan to impress actress Jodie Foster, on whom he had a deranged crush. And there in a way you have the progression of idealism in the American assassin.

In the photographs of Lincoln's first inaugural four years earlier, on March 4, 1861, what looms above and behind him is not the skulking killer, but scaffolding. They were still building the Capitol. When the war broke out, construction halted, but Lincoln, who knew the value of symbols, ordered work to resume as evidence for all to see that "the Union shall go on." Let's go inside now, to the Great Rotunda.

Rotundas impart a feeling of drama, even if you're shuffling through along with 200 high schoolers from Terre Haute, Indiana. It's an amazing space. The floor is Aquia Creek sandstone worn so smooth you want to take your shoes off and feel it on your soles. (Caution: don't— they'll think you're a shoe bomber.) During the Civil War, this same space, unfinished, served as a barracks for the Eighth Massachusetts Regiment. In the cellars beneath, 150 bakers turned out 60,000 loaves a day for the Union

Army. I'll resist the temptation to say that seldom has the Capitol been put to more productive use.

You'll get a stiff neck peering up at Constantino Brumidi's fresco, *Apotheosis of Washington,* 180 feet above in the dome's canopy. Not just any apotheosis, but a 4,664-square-foot apotheosis. To a republican (small r), it seems a tad grandiose, showing Washington in excelsis, seated with the Goddess of Liberty on the right and Victory and Fame on his left. But then apotheoses tend not to be exercises in modesty.

Washington had long since ascended to Olympus by the time Brumidi painted it, between 1865 and 1866, and it's just as well, since he probably would have taken one look at it and ordered it wallpapered over. He was not without vanity, old George, but as a good Deist (God as indifferent Clockmaker), apotheosis wasn't really his thing. He turned down a third term, he didn't want the Federal City named after him, and he didn't even want L'Enfant's equestrian statue. John Adams asked the widow Washington if they could move his remains here. She agreed, but 30 years later when the central structure of the Capitol was ready for his crypt, a nephew refused, and so he remains at Mount Vernon. Perhaps it's just as well. The nephew's demurral may have saved the Capitol from becoming a grandiose tomb like the *Invalides* in Paris, where Napoleon's remains lie in a sepulchre that looks like it was designed for—well, Napoleon. Turning the Capitol into a giant tomb would subtly alter the essence of the thing. Imagine the dismal image of all those senators and congressmen invoking the hallowed corpse below by way of justifying raising the tariff on Caribbean sugar.

If you've brought binoculars with you, check out the woman with the sword hovering beneath the godlike Washington: it's rumored to be Brumidi's mistress. Brumidi was an elfin Italian with a Victorian Vandyke and naughty-old-man eyes. He spent almost a quarter-century in this building painting heroic frescoes and friezes, and was once left dangling 60 feet above the Rotunda floor after falling off the scaffolding. He eventually died of the shock and strain. It's not everyone's cup of tea. In *The Gilded Age,* Mark Twain declared the interior of the Capitol to be a "delerium tremens of art." He had a point, but you can't say that it's not really representative.

I'll let you prowl about. There's a lot to see: the Old Senate Chamber, Statuary Hall, the Crypt, the Old Supreme Court Chamber, the Hall of Columns, along with enough murals, portraits, busts, and bas reliefs to keep you going "Huh" for hours. Meantime, as we leave the Great Rotunda, I'll note that the first president to lie in state in this chamber was Lincoln. He was the only president who was inaugurated both in an incomplete and completed Capitol Building. In those four years he saw to the finishing of something else: the United States.

Someone else of note lay in state in this room—Major Pierre Charles L'Enfant. The headline from the *Evening Star* of April 28, 1909, reads:

HONOR TO L'ENFANT
TARDY BUT SINCERE

He had been moldering away in his pauper's grave out near Bladensburg since 1825. By 1909 it had become a bit embarrassing. His casket was draped in an American flag and floral arrangements and guarded, fittingly, by sergeants of the U.S. Army Corps of Engineers. President and Mrs. Taft were in attendance, along with the French ambassador, M. Jusserand. Vice President Sherman was moved to speak in couplets: "He gazed into the future far as human eye could see. /And saw the beauty of the spot and all the grandeur that would be." Congress immediately passed a law prohibiting vice presidents from speaking in verse; it remains on the books today.

It was one named Henry B. F. Macfarland, president of the board of directors of the District of Columbia, who put it best, but I'll save that for when we come to L'Enfant's final resting place. The cortege that left the Great Rotunda that day, by the time it had assembled fully, stretched for an entire mile.

GRANT MEMORIAL

I wanted to check out the view seen by Ronald Reagan—and Bill Clinton and George Bush, father and son—when they took the oath of office, but this was post 9/11 and the Capitol Hill police were unimpressed by my need to access the West Front. It's a shame, what's happened: metal detectors, Jersey barriers, streets closed, suspicious stares from once-friendly police, ACCESS DENIED signs where once you could breeze through. In Lincoln's day, security was so casual that people used to steal the White House doorknobs. But now we're embarked on some version of a Hundred Years War, and if it hadn't been for some brave passengers on Flight 93 that day, this entire building with its gleaming dome might have been reduced to a blackened heap, so let us count our blessings.

I walked down the slope of what was once Jenkins Hill toward the Mall. It was a warm day and a platoon of bare-chested marines from the nearby barracks were doing abdominal crunches on the grass. I remember years ago attending a twilight parade at the Marine Barracks in honor of the vice president, an impressive demonstration of marching and precision drilling, marines tossing bayonet-fixed rifles within inches of each other's noses. Arriving here from New York, I was struck by the presence everywhere of soldiers. Where I came from, they were a rare sight. Now if you see a miniconvoy of camo-painted Hummers mounted with .50-caliber guns roaring through Times Square, it's both alarming and reassuring.

I heard what sounded like Scripture being spoken over a PA system. The Mall is America's most public space, a vast version of Speakers' Corner near Marble Arch in London's Hyde Park. Anyone can come—and generally does, sometimes in large numbers—to make his or her views abundantly clear.

The sound was emanating from a group of women who were convening here from all corners of the nation for the National Day of Prayer. They had begun reading the Bible at eight A.M. on Monday. It was now two P.M. on Wednesday, and they had been going nonstop. "We're just getting to Jeremiah," a church lady in summer dress and straw hat cheerfully told me. I wished her well and continued on. Behind me I heard through the loudspeakers, "I shall be your lawyer, to plead your case, and I shall avenge you!" An apt bit of the Good Book to cite in a city where every third inhabitant seems to be a lawyer.

At the foot of the hill I stumbled upon the Grant Memorial, if you can truly "stumble" upon a 252-foot-long memorial. I'm embarrassed to say that I didn't even know it was there. I grew up in New York City, where Grant is buried and all we did was make jokes about the fact. ("Who's buried in Grant's tomb?") I visited the tomb once, to find that it had been turned into a combination *pissoir* and shooting gallery for bums and drug addicts. *"Look on my works, ye Mighty, and despair!"* said Ozymandias.

There's something about Grant, despite his key contribution to our history, that seems to keep nudging him away from the limelight. His presidency, probably. But there are reasons to stop here and pay our respects. First, it's a memorial not to the president, but to the general who saved the Union.

For a heroic-scale monument, it's entirely unheroic. Grant sits atop his horse, Cincinnatus, with his hat slouched over his forehead, looking as though he's just been informed that he's lost 7,000 men.

During battles, Grant usually stayed in his tent—not because he was a coward. On the contrary, he was all guts, as his last days proved, when, dying of throat cancer, he refused pain medication so that he could finish writing his memoirs, the royalties from which he hoped would sustain his family after he was gone. His business partners had managed to bankrupt the family. His memoirs ended up earning $450,000—about $8,200,000 today, even more than the $6.5 million advance paid to General Colin Powell for his autobiography in the mid-1990s. The critic Edmund Wilson, a notably tough grader, pronounced Grant's memoirs the best military memoirs since Caesar's *Commentaries.* Grant stayed in his tent lest he be swayed by the sight of all the bloodshed and ghastly suffering. He was afraid to flinch. He was a classic hedgehog, to use the Greek poet Archilochus's formulation about how the fox knows many small things, but the hedgehog knows one large thing. Grant knew what needed to be done. And did it.

As a result of that single-mindedness, the president whose memorial sits two miles west of here at the opposite end of this vast lawn was able to win the war and save the Union. Grant and Lincoln book-end the Mall. Grant is facing Lincoln, but he's also facing beyond, to his old enemy Robert E. Lee's house atop the hill in Arlington National Cemetery. And he stands at the foot of Capitol

Hill, defending the building behind him that symbolized the Union.

The second reason to pay our respects here is that Grant drank and smoked, and it seems apt, in neo-Temperance times, to celebrate a man who could win a war while occasionally going on benders and smoking 20 cigars a day. It's been quoted to death, but it's worth repeating: Lincoln, assailed by hand-wringers over Grant's drinking, famously replied, "If I knew what brand of whiskey he drinks I would send a barrel or so to some other generals."

A third reason to doff our hats is that, had it not been for Grant's patronage of a man named Alexander "Boss" Shepherd, we might be holding handkerchiefs over our faces as we stand on this spot, or, more likely, be fleeing back uphill, away from the awful stench.

Appointed by Grant, Shepherd governed Washington in the 1870s. As with many of Grant's associates, he was a bit careless about the bottom line, but he got things done. And a lot needed doing. When Shepherd took over, Washington was in terrible shape as the result of having served as a military campground during the Civil War. The streets were mud, disease was rampant. The term "Third World" hadn't yet been coined, but it if had, Washington would have been smack in the middle of it.

One of the first things Shepherd did was to fill in Tiber Creek and the canal it connected to that ran right past this spot at the foot of Capitol Hill. The Tiber and canal were basically open sewers. Butchers from the Central Market used to dump carcasses into it. Imagine what *that* smelled like around, say, July. Lincoln slept at the Soldier's Home, three miles north, whenever he could, just to escape the miasmas.

Shepherd paved the streets, lit them, built parks, tore down old buildings, ripped up railroad tracks, planted 60,000 trees, and installed water and sewer systems. He did this "with czarlike zeal" according to the Works Project Administration guide to D.C. To my way of thinking, this qualifies him as a great man, if not an outright saint. Yet poor Shepherd is mainly pointed out these days for having run up a $22 million deficit. The evil that men do lives after them; the good is oft interred with their sewer pipes. Shepherd seems to have had a sense of humor: he named his mansion "Bleak House" because he read Dickens's novel while he was building it. At any rate, pause by Cincinnatus's hooves and be grateful to Boss Shepherd that you're not gagging. His story has a rare happy ending: having gone broke, he fled to Mexico, where he took over an old mine, discovered gold and silver, became a millionaire again, returned, and was given a great big parade down Pennsylvania Avenue. Less happy is the fact that the sculptor of this vast and haunting memorial, Henry Merwin Shrady, who worked on it for 20 years, died of exhaustion two weeks before it was unveiled. Shrady's father was the doctor who attended to the general in his last great battle, with the cancer, so much is owed to both Shradys.

NATIONAL GALLERY OF ART—EAST BUILDING

Now that we've contemplated heroic sculpture of the Beaux Arts era, let's wander over to the East Building of the National Gallery of Art to admire the latest minimalist installations. Perhaps the Brooklyn Museum of Art has loaned them an elephant-dung Madonna or two.

Sorry, couldn't resist. Let me quickly assert that I love the East Building, even if I'm a hopeless philistine who doesn't and probably never will "get" gigantic Motherwell canvases. Maybe I could if he just titled them *Overpriced Ink Blot* #7. At any rate, the East Building is Washington's answer to New York's Guggenheim Museum: the funnest—as my then seven-year-old daughter called it on her first visit—space in town.

There was a trustees' meeting going on the day I was there, and outside were parked the finest German, Japanese, and British cars that American money can buy. The sound of applause periodically wafted out from the meeting room and fell, like aural leaves, to the stone.

Andrew W. Mellon—lawyer-judge-banker, founder of Alcoa, U.S. Steel, Gulf Oil too, ambassador to Great Britain and secretary of the treasury under Harding, Coolidge, and Hoover—gave us the National Gallery of Art. His son Paul gave us this in 1978, at a cost of $95 million. Architect I. M. Pei created it: two very nonconventional triangles of pink Tennessee marble with more edges than a Swiss army knife, more angles than an Enron partnership, and more intersecting planes than an M. C. Escher etching. Let's go inside.

The interior is dominated by an enormous multi-colored Alexander Calder mobile. The guide told us that it is meant to "suggest nature motifs and to offset the triangularity of the building." That sounded about right. But let me add a more scholarly gloss: to me it suggests everything that colossal art can be, uplifting the soul with a loud gleeful, "Wheeeee!" If ever the world becomes too much with you and you find yourself reaching for the pill bottle or noose, come down here and sit a while underneath Mr. Calder's mobile. Then for heaven's sake, get proper medical help. But if the mobile fails to soothe, the Zen garden might, with its cool gravel rakings. If you're feeling depressed, do try to avoid the Andy Warhol self-portrait. That will not help. I came upon it accidentally while going up some steps and fell into a severe melancholy for several hours.

NATIONAL GALLERY OF ART— WEST BUILDING

We're going to take the tunnel, so don't walk out the door, but before we descend, do admire Pei's glass tetrahedrons rising out of the scalloped granite cobblestone plaza between the two buildings. There's something about venerable old art galleries like this one and the Louvre in Paris that make Pei cry out, "Glass tetrahedrons!" It's his version of slip-covering everything. At first this causes severe harrumphing among the conservative element, but in the end people just love them. And they do admit lots of light into the lower levels. The savings on lightbulbs must be huge.

We're going to pause in the Cascade Café underneath the pyramids and have a spot of lunch. I don't know about you, but I'm famished. If we're lucky, we'll get a seat by the waterfall, where we can watch the water tumbling over the rocks, without a worry in the world about the basement flooding.

I had the chicken roll-up and mint tea. What did you have? The food here is wonderful and varied. Ready? Let's continue, then.

To get from one building to the other, they cleverly make you walk through a gauntlet of museum gift shops, where you can buy everything from Van Gogh umbrellas to 25-pound books on German expressionism—the perfect Christmas gift for a boss you don't really like. Pause briefly to consider what Van Gogh would make of the umbrella. Would he chop off the other ear? There's an art history Ph.D. dissertation I'd read.

Coming up into the main entryway of the West Building and continuing on up the stairs, we find ourselves, once again, beneath a coffered dome, as we did in the Capitol. You just can't escape domes in any capital city. But this one's another beauty, and the oculus at the top might remind you of the one in the Pantheon in Rome, the only original Roman temple still in use (albeit as a Christian church).

The graceful bronze statue of Mercury at the center—"New lighted on a heaven-kissing hill," as Hamlet said to his mother, Gertrude, after stabbing Polonius behind the arras—depicts the god in his manifestation as symbol of the FTD, the florists' telegraph delivery service. Its sculptor, Francesco Righetti, modeled it after an earlier version by Giovanni Bologna, who captured Mercury at the moment of delivering a dozen yellow roses to the wrong address in Fort Lauderdale. Note the hint of *terribilità* in the god's demeanor, reminiscent, perhaps, of Ghiberti's almost fanatic neo-plasticism, auguring in a new dialectic between the Flemish linearism of the north and the *soppressata* of the gouache Guelphs of the Ligurian littoral. Or perhaps not.

Some of those self-guided audio museum tours can sound a bit like that, narrated by curators in urgent need of adenoidectomy. Not here. The narration is down-to-earth, to the point, piquant even, and without a mote of condescension. There are about 1,000 paintings in the West Building, and the good news is that we will not be looking at all of them today. Instead, we will opt to take the "Director's Tour," the audio tour. Deep down, I suspect another name would be "Our Best Stuff Tour," but they'd probably never admit to it. At any rate, it's well worth the five bucks. You will feel a bit odd walking from room to room with the audio thing pressed to the side of your head like an Edwardian ear-trumpet, but you get used to it.

Since this is a book about America's capital city, my plan was to concentrate on the American galleries, but I got a bit sidetracked. A lifetime of going to the Frick Collection in New York City (still, I confess, my favorite museum) led me ineluctably to the Bouchers and Fragonards, entitled, respectively, *The Love Letter* and *The Swing*. Talleyrand wrote that those who had not been alive before the French Revolution could not truly know what it was to experience *la douceur de vivre,* the sweetness of life. (*"Aucun homme n'en pouvait apprécier 'la douceur de vivre' s'il n'avait pas déjà vécu avant 1789."*) These paintings give a clue as to just how very *doux* it was: blessed-out young aristos gamboling in ripe gardens (while the peasants were huddling in the city eating rotting vegetables and sharpening the guillotine blade). Looking at these pretty young things, you just know they're about to rush into the bushes and pull up those petticoats and have *incroyable* sex. Why, you wonder, would L'Enfant have left this lush Arcadie behind to come freeze his *noisettes* at Valley Forge fighting for a bunch of smelly *Américains?* Perhaps he was, how do you say, prescient? Then there's Boucher's *Venus Consoling Love,* which was commissioned by the marquise de Pompadour, mistress of Louis XV—for her bathroom. It's well not to linger here too long. Bad for the heart.

Okay, the Americans. Our moment! Thomas Cole's four allegorical paintings (1842) on the theme of "The Voyage of Life" have their own room, as well they should. They depict the trip as experienced by a man in a boat going down a river: Childhood, Youth, Manhood, Old Age—three stages less than Shakespeare enumerated in Act I, Scene 7 of *As You Like It.* Today Cole would have to add two other stages: "Viagra Falls" and "Assisted Living."

Now we come to the inner temple of aesthetic Americana: the Gilbert Stuarts. Stuart—this you already knew—did not get along with his most famous subject, Washington. Poor George—between Stuart and L'Enfant, temperamental artists on all sides. Stuart was the Yousuf Karsh of his day, Karsh being the Ottawa photographic portraitist who famously plucked Churchill's cigar out of his hand moments before snapping the shutter, an act of *lèse-majesté* that produced the famous photograph of the glowering, formidable Last Lion, grumbling, *Give me back my Romeo y Julieta Montecristo, you upstart wog!* Washington's lips are pursed tightly around his hippopotamus tooth dentures, his left eye boring into the viewer with such frigid intensity as to make one grateful never to have been subject to such majestic displeasure. Stuart despaired of making the great man relax. According to Washington's current biographer, Richard Brookhiser, he tried to jolly Washington by prattling on, telling amusing stories and anecdotes. Washington, however, was not someone to be jollied. All Stuart's gambits did was make him clamp down even tighter on those hippo choppers and lower the temperature of that left eyeball another 10 degrees Fahrenheit. Stuart commented to others that Washington had "a temper." Henry Lee related this to Mrs. Washington, who complained that this was impertinent, whereupon her husband the president remarked, "Stuart is right." He may have been a bit of a stick, our Father, but he was self-aware.

In the same room, we find Stuart's portrait of the other American gods: a Micawberesque John Adams (the one on the cover of David McCullough's best-selling biography); a rather prim Jefferson; a puffy Madison; and serene, blue-eyed Monroe.

Here's Copley's *Watson and the Shark,* the "Jaws" of its day (1778). In our sensory-overloaded era, it's hard to appreciate just how dramatic a painting like this must have been at the time, with the open-jawed, razor-toothed shark closing in on Watson's ghost-white body. Watson lost half his leg to the brute in Havana harbor at the age of 14. But he had grown up in an orphanage and wasn't about to let this hold him back in life: he became a successful businessman and even Lord Mayor of London. He commissioned the painting and gave it to the Christ's Hospital, a boys' school, where it might serve as a "most usefull Lesson to Youth." It would have been a useful lesson to this youth—never to set a pinkie in Havana harbor. When we get to Lafayette Square we will meet another colorful fellow who delighted in his own amputation.

America got a late start in painting, but to wander through these rooms it appears that we got up to speed quickly: Albert Bierstadt's *Lake Lucerne* (1858) with its dramatic alps and icy green water; George Caleb Bingham's Huck Finn–like *The Jolly Flatboatmen* (1846); Frederic Church's 70-millimeter wide-screen Technicolor extravaganza, *Morning in the Tropics* (1877). Church used to charge admission for his paintings, and their openings were as eagerly anticipated as movie premieres are today.

The true American masterpieces—not that I'm remotely qualified to pronounce them so—are surely, *must* be, the George Catlins from the 1840s of Indian chiefs and medicine men and buffalo hunters. No artist has caught the inner nobility of the Red Man as he did. (NOTE TO P.C. POLICE: they *are* Red.) To contemplate these magnificent creatures is to mourn the genocide that we visited on them. Pause a moment to honor them and offer a prayer for forgiveness. (We'll be doing a lot of this later on at the Holocaust Museum, only there we get to be angry at Germans.)

Just one or two more: Winslow Homer's *Hound and Hunter* (1892) manages to be both dramatic and hilarious at the same time, showing a boy in his canoe struggling desperately to keep the six-point buck that he has just shot from sinking to the bottom of the river. And *Right and Left,* Homer's last great picture, done in 1909. It's the one showing two ducks being shot over water. The audio tour says this was a "premonition of his own mortality," but then adds nicely that "its first owner was interested in it as a piece of hunting art." That's what the rich hunters I know would have taken away from it. My Canadian grandfather's idea of Fine Art consisted of a hunting dog fetching a quail. Meanwhile, look closely above the wave in the distance and you'll see a little orange flash of the hunter's shotgun muzzle. To get that detail right, Homer had a friend row out in a boat and shoot blanks at him.

If you want a little shot of vitamin P (Patriotism) on our way out, you could stand in front of Childe Hassam's *Allies Day, May 1917,* showing New York's Fifth Avenue, as vibrantly as it has ever been with the red, white, and blue of the American and French flags flapping away on a sparkling spring day. You'd hardly suspect that it was all, ultimately, about a war that consumed millions of young men in muddy trenches fouled by poison gas. A year into the Great War, someone asked the Kaiser what it was about. He replied, "I wish to God I knew."

That's enough art for now, and we didn't even look at the Rubens and Rembrandts. They did a study before they built the East Building in the late 1970s that revealed that the average museum goer's attention span is 45 minutes, so they designed the East Building with that in mind. You could spend 45 years in the West Building.

Meantime, mustn't bog down. Why don't you put your feet up in one of the lovely Garden Courts, and refresh and recharge amid the fronds and fountains and meet me in the lobby downstairs in, say, 10 minutes? As you wait, a story to muse on as you relax in the cool greenery:

You're sitting in the space once occupied by the Baltimore and Potomac Railroad Station. It was here, on July 2, 1881, that the deranged office-seeker Charles Guiteau shot President James Garfield. Garfield was on his way to his 25th reunion at Williams College. The president was accompanied by Abraham Lincoln's son, Robert Todd Lincoln. Hold on to that thought—we'll discuss this further when we get to Arlington Cemetery. The reason I'm telling you all this is on the chance that it's hot today.

Poor old Garfield lingered until September 19. To keep him as comfortable as they could, while he lay dying of blood poisoning—not from the bullets, but in all likelihood from the probings of the doctors' dirty fingers—navy technicians were tasked with improvising an early form of air conditioning, consisting of a fan blowing air over blocks of ice. (George Washington was similarly abused by his doctors as he lay dying of acute bacterial epiglottitis in 1799, as they thrust their grubby fingers down his gullet trying to clear his airway; they also drained the poor man of most of his blood.)

The long, lingering death of Garfield is especially poignant to anyone who has spent a summer in Washington, D.C. Finally, in September, they put him on a train for the New Jersey seacoast so that his final agonies would at least be mitigated by the ocean air. They even built a special train track right up to his front door. Be grateful for air conditioning and latex gloves. Later on, we'll see the device used by Alexander Graham Bell to try to locate the bullets inside Garfield.

I was going to take you to the National Archives. But it's closed for repairs. It should be open again by the time you read this. The building is another neo-classical John Russell Pope temple (he also did the building we're just about to leave, as well as the Jefferson Memorial). As a writer, it's nice to consider that two of the most impressive buildings in Washington are the Library of Congress and the Archives. Walking up the steps into the Archives would make even a great writer feel puny and insignificant. (Though not Gore Vidal.) To see those Founding documents, in their nuclear bomb–proof cases, is humbling. *We hold these truths to be self-evident, that all men are created equal . . .* the words have not lost their power to raise the hairs on the arms. But let me tell you about some other words I once saw on display here.

At the end of World War II, General Eisenhower gathered his top aides and generously invited them to help him compose the cable announcing the end of the war. They took up their pens and came up with the most purple, flowery, self-consciously dramatic declarations. You can imagine the emotions that were going on in the room among these commanders who had just prevailed in the greatest conflict in history. Ike looked over their submissions, politely thanked them, and then sat down and wrote it out himself in pencil: "The mission of this Allied Force was fulfilled at 0241, local time, May 7th, 1945." A few years ago I saw that piece of paper here. It was one of the most moving documents I've ever seen.

Okay, let's hit the Mall.

NATIONAL AIR AND SPACE MUSEUM

Crossing to the National Air and Space Museum is a chance to appreciate the enormity and simplicity of this lawn. It didn't always look like this. Until the McMillan Commission came along at the turn of the century, it was a Victorian tangle of winding paths and gardens and shady arbors, no doubt pleasant to perambulate about in, but no more distinctive than many other city parks. Then Frederick Law Olmsted put on his gardener's gloves and went to work on what might as well have been called "The Great Tidying Up of 1901." The result is what you see: a grand—perhaps a tad grandiose; it *is* rather imperial—*allée* stretching two miles all the way to the river, in keeping with L'Enfant's original idea. Only in L'Enfant's time, the land ended just west of where the Washington Monument is. Everything south of the Monument was once river. A capital built on landfill—now *there's* a metaphor.

Before we go inside the most popular museum in the country, I'll briefly note the fact that it stands pretty much on the site of what was once one of Washington's largest and most successful bawdy houses. It was owned by a woman named Mary Ann Hall. "She had a *great* location," noted the guide whose tour I joined one day, "right next to the Congress. This was during the Civil War, so it must have been an exhausting time for Mrs. Hall's ladies. The word *hooker*—as you already know—is eponymous, deriving from the name of the general who rounded up the city's numerous prostitutes and bivouacked them in one area so that they could be more easily kept under surveillance. They became known collectively as Hooker's Division. The area where he parked them became, not surprisingly, the city's preeminent red light district. They were quartered on the northern side of the Mall, where the Federal Triangle of government offices now sits, or squats, or whatever it is a Federal Triangle does. At any rate, this quondam pleasure center is now the site of the Internal Revenue Service, the Justice and Commerce Departments, Federal Trade Commission, Ronald Reagan Building, and International Trade Center. But turning back to the Air and Space Museum, how apt it is that the land once occupied by Mrs. Hall's establishment is still dedicated, one way or another, to sending man to the moon.

Walk into the National Air and Space Museum through the Mall entrance and you find yourself in a cathedral-like area occupied by every significant relic of aviation history, from the Wright Brothers' 1903 *Flyer* to the *Apollo 11* command module *Columbia*. Less than 70 years elapsed between the flights of those two craft. Almost half that amount of time has now elapsed since Neil Armstrong landed on the moon, which prompts one to wonder if our great adventure hasn't somehow stalled. I say this with all due respect, indeed awe, for the bravery and endurance of the astronauts who are up there almost every day assembling the space station and studying the effects of weightlessness on the mating habits of fruit flies. And to the wizards who direct space probes through unimaginable distances. But the last time we all really focused on space was when the *Challenger* exploded in 1986. The latest headline from the space front is that the Russians have agreed (for a $20 million fee) to send a member of the rock band N'Sync into space. This is not quite up there with "The Eagle has landed." Looking at the *Apollo* capsule here with its scorched underside takes you back to the happier time of July 1969, the last time the entire world stopped everything it was doing and held its breath, face to face, to paraphrase from the last lines of *The Great Gatsby,* for the last time in history with something commensurate to its capacity for wonder.

Look around this space. It's the ultimate boy's bedroom, the most historical aircraft in history hanging from the ceiling: Lindbergh's *Spirit of St. Louis;* the *Bell X-1* ("Glamorous Glennis") in which Chuck Yeager broke the sound barrier in 1947; a replica of *Sputnik 1,* the Russian satellite that gave the West a major case of the willies in 1957 and started us in earnest toward the moon. Mounted on the floor is a model of Goddard's first liquid-propellent rocket from *Mercury Friendship 7,* the capsule that carried John Glenn three times around the world in 1962. To match this, an art museum would have to hang in one large room the Elgin Marbles, *Guernica,* Monet's *Water Lilies,* the *Mona Lisa, Last Supper,* and—of course—Motherwell's *Overpriced Ink Blot #7.*

To one side, standing like two malevolent phalli, are a Soviet SS-20 intermediate-range ballistic nuclear missile and its counterpart, a U.S. Pershing-II. If *Apollo 11* once brought us all together, these bloody things almost put us asunder—and for good—and in this fierce drama I played a teensy part.

The last trip I made with Vice President Bush, to Europe in February of 1983, was to urge the Europeans to stop moaning and wringing their hands over the deployment of the Pershings—a deployment that they had requested in the first place, in order to counterbalance the deployment by the Soviets of hundreds of their SS-20s. (The Cuban missiles that almost caused World War III in 1962 were SS-4s.) What had the Europeans biting their nails down to the cuticles—apart from their natural inclination to do this—was the idea that these were so-called theater nuclear weapons; that is, they were targeted to land all over Europe, but not on Russian or U.S. soil. Mr. Bush was duly dispatched to calm our allies.

It was a tense time. It has subsequently become known that the Russians actually believed that Reagan might launch nuclear weapons at their "evil empire." During our trip, *Air Force Two* was awash in top secret documents about Soviet capabilities and intelligence reports.

One night, blearily reworking speech number whatever, I found stuck to the speech text that I had circulated a most thrilling TOP SECRET CODEWORD EYES ONLY document. The very cream of confidentiality! It had been mistakenly paper-clipped to my returned speech text. I can tell you this now because it no longer matters. It was a list of code words to be used in nonsecure telephone conversations between the vice president and the White House. Thus Mr. Bush would be able to conduct a coherent conversation on a phone monitored by Soviet intelligence, and they wouldn't know what the hell he was talking about. The Soviets had bugs everywhere, and, as it turned out, high-level moles at the CIA and the FBI.

The subject matter being referred to in this list of code words was jaw-droppingly sensitive: dual-key launch of nuclear weapons. We were—apparently—prepared to mollify our European allies by means of the following protocol: two keys, one U.S., one French or German or Italian, would be required to launch a Pershing missile. That way, it wouldn't be a unilateral American decision. I suspect this was actually just a feint, and that if push ever came to shove, our own key would be sufficient to, in the words of *Dr. Strangelove*'s General Buck Turgidson, "Blast off!" But this was apparently the compromise we were prepared to make in order to ensure those missiles were deployed.

To a 29-year-old hack writer such as myself doing a White House gig, this was heady stuff. President Reagan was "Mr. Robinson," Soviet General Secretary Andropov was "Mr. Baxter." France was "Indiana," Italy "Pennsylvania." SS-20s were "chopsticks," Pershings "Buicks." And so forth. I imagined the vice president and the director of national security having this bizarre-sounding conversation. Simpler, I suppose, than bringing the Navajo windtalkers out of retirement. At any rate, it was all tip-top secret—and the person on our trip entrusted with this nuclear Rosetta cribsheet had managed, inadvertently, to place it in the hands of—the speech writer.

I did not particularly like the fellow. He had that attitude, not uncommon among his brethren, of condescending to anyone below his technical rank, and in his evolutionary food chain, I was about one grade up from paramecium. But now I had the only copy of his precious codes. Wheeeee! I pondered how to maximize upon this gorgeous bit of luck.

I decided to share my wealth. I went to Admiral Daniel J. Murphy, the former four-star admiral who was the vice president's chief of staff. Dan had aviated in World War II, Korea, and the Cold War, and had commanded the Sixth Fleet in the Mediterranean during the 1973–74 Arab-Israeli war. He was no shrinking violet when it came to the great bureaucratic game. And since our trip had begun, even he had been subject to a certain amount of peckerflexing by Mr. Code Word.

I handed Dan the sheet of paper. How his eyes did widen. He looked at me. I looked at him. We refrained from high-fiving.

Within an hour, Mr. Code Word's attitude underwent a remarkable transformation. Moreover, it remained transformed for the duration of our nine-city swing through Europe. Indeed, he became the soul of collegiality and deference. I've never spoken of this until now.

Dan Murphy died on September 21, 2001. He was a great American, and a good and decent man, and even though he could scare the crap out of me, I was proud to serve under him. As for Mr. Code Word, he now occupies a position of mind-boggling power, and seems to be doing an able job at it. I doubt he's misplaced any paper clips since.

The trip through Europe was a success. George Bush was superb. The Europeans calmed down. The Pershings were deployed. The Russians concluded that the United States would not back down, and a few years later President Reagan was shouting, "Mr. Gorbachev, tear down this wall!" and it was all over. And that's how I won the Cold War.

A few weeks after I visited the Air and Space Museum to scribble my notes, I went back with my wife to attend a party there on the 75th anniversary of Charles Lindbergh's flight. Our hostess was Reeve Lindbergh, his daughter, author of several wonderful children's books, including *The Midnight Farm*. Reeve Lindbergh has a radiant, warm face crinkled with laugh lines. She looks very much like her beautiful mother, Anne Morrow Lindbergh, author of the classic book *Gift from the Sea*. Her father, Dwight Morrow, was a distinguished U.S. ambassador to Mexico and once gave asylum to my paternal grandfather after he had backed the wrong revolution down there and found himself temporarily inconvenienced by a sentence of death.

Senator John Glenn reminisced onstage about being a young marine pilot in the Pacific, and how Charles Lindbergh had one day arrived at their air base to advise the squadron on how to cope with some of the design peculiarities of their Lockheed P-38 Lightning. The plane had a huge prop that caused severe torque problems, a tail wheel that caused it to career to the left after landing, and a canopy "you couldn't see out of. Otherwise," said Mr. Glenn, "it was a great plane." And here was Charles Lindbergh, the most famous aviator in history, to help them figure it out.

Listening to a god of my youth—in 1962 I watched spellbound as Glenn made his record-breaking three orbits—talking about the god of his youth was one of those exercises in connecting the historical dots.

Afterward, there was a buffet supper in the great room with all those planes and spacecraft. I chatted with a man from Philadelphia whose grandfather had been a guest of U.S. Ambassador Myron T. Herrick in Paris on May 21, 1927. Herrick had asked him if he would like to accompany him to Le Bourget airfield to welcome this young American aviator. His grandfather had said, No, no, I have a golf game all arranged, thanks just the same.

My wife nudged me and pointed to a posse of Lindbergh's great-great-grandchildren climbing over *Friendship 7* as if it were a playground choo-choo. A band played 1920s songs, including the "Lindy Hop." Eighty-two-year-old Norma Miller, an elegant black lady all in silver glitter who had popularized that song, sang on a stage in front of the scorched underside of *Apollo 11*'s *Columbia.* Above it all hung *Spirit of St. Louis,* still aloft 75 years later, still headed toward Paris.

Let's exit by the same door we entered and turn left. A block later, you may feel as though you are under observation by Big Brother, or about to be fired upon from the world's largest pillbox. Remain calm. It's only the . . .

HIRSHHORN MUSEUM AND SCULPTURE GARDEN

By "only," I don't mean to belittle it. Joseph Hirshhorn would have dazzled Horatio Alger. He arrived from Latvia at the age of six and ended up owning most of the world's uranium. The man loved art: he amassed maybe the world's largest private collection of it, 4,000 paintings and 2,000 sculptures. If you amass this much art, sooner or later you're going to need a place to put it. And here it all is, inside this building called, informally, "the Donut."

I don't think that the nickname adequately conveys the sense of fear and panic it inspires in the casual stroller. According to E. J. Applewhite's *Washington Itself,* the Donut's architect was Gordon Bunshaft, who designed New York City's Lever House, Chase Manhattan Bank on Wall Street, and 9 West 57th, the skyscraper with the curved side sloping down to that giant red number 9 sculpture on the sidewalk that I always manage to walk into after too many vodkas at the Russian Tea Room.

There was a kafuffle over building the Hirshhorn. There's always a kafuffle when it comes to putting something on the Mall. Just wait till we get to the Vietnam Veterans Memorial. At any rate, S. Dillon Ripley, secretary of the Smithsonian from 1964 to 1984, struck a deal with the Uranium King: you give us the art, and we'll put your museum on the Mall. Mr. Hirshhorn wanted it next to the Archives, and he wanted the sculpture garden to extend all the way across the Mall. These bold demands were— thank heavens—ix-nayed. Then he wanted it to be made of Italian marble, but there's a rule that government buildings can't be made out of furreign material. A committee was duly appointed to determine the ugliest native material that money could buy and to construct the Donut out of that.

I'm piling on here. I don't mean to be ungrateful to Mr. Hirshhorn. Anyway, here it all is, and over to you. I should mention what used to be here, from 1887 to 1969: the Army Medical Museum. That's now located at Walter Reed Hospital. It was here that a leg amputated during the Civil War was placed on display, and every year, on the anniversary of the amputation, its former owner would come, friends in tow, to visit it. We'll hear more about this later when we get to Lafayette Square. Meanwhile, moving right along, on our left (if you exit the Hirshhorn on the Mall side) we come to the . . .

SMITHSONIAN

Technically, we come first to the Arts and Industries Building, a gay old pile built in the 1880s as America's way of proclaiming, "We're not just a bunch of heavily armed farmers. We know all about this Industrial Revolution thing." It was here that President Garfield's inaugural ball was held, four months before Guiteau nailed him at the B&P depot several hundred yards across the Mall.

Okay, now we do come to the Smithsonian Institution building, the nation's attic. The "Castle," as it's called, was the first building on the Mall (1855) and it looks it. The *WPA Guide* describes it nicely as "a confusion of towers, turrets, and pinnacles" in an "adaptation of Lombard and

Norman styles." It's the sort of building we call "venerable" without actually wanting to live in it. I wouldn't. I have a rule about living in buildings that have active sarcophagi in the foyer.

This is where Mr. James Smithson is buried. He was an English scientist who never visited the United States, until his corpse did after being parked in a cemetery in Genoa, Italy, for 75 years. The Italian authorities were going to demolish the cemetery, so we dispatched Alexander Graham Bell to pick him up.

Smithson was the illegitimate son of the Duke of Northumberland. He amassed a fortune—remember, to end up on the Mall, you must first "amass" a "fortune" in uranium, minerals, steel, whatever—and left it all, amounting to about $500,000 (about $9,400,000 today) to the United States, for an "establishment for the increase and diffusion of knowledge among men." (In those days, you could safely leave out "and women.") The condition was that if his sole survivor, a nephew, produced an heir, the deal was off. There must have been a lot of nail-biting about the nephew's testosterone levels. Fortunately, the nephew died without issue.

John C. Calhoun took time out from championing slavery to rage against accepting the gift, on the grounds that it was a constitutional violation of states' rights to accept gifts from furreigners, and, worse, demeaning to the dignity of the United States. Only 15 years had passed since Rear Admiral Cockburn and his merry band of incendiaries had passed through, so some in the Congress were still feeling a little burned. It was John Quincy Adams, being a cultured Bostonian, who grasped that we were never going to get any respect from Europe unless we increased and diffused what learning we had. He pushed the deal through. Having solved the stink about taking money from furreigners, they proceeded to build a completely furreign-looking castle.

The statue in front is of the Smithsonian's first secretary, Joseph Henry. If you look at the pedestal, you'll see an electromagnet. Dr. Henry was the spiritual godfather of the Weather Channel: he was the first to point out the merits of telegraphing the next town over the news that a tornado has just removed your roof and Aunt Hattie.

I'd tell you about James Smithson's ghost, but we have lots more to see and should probably be getting on. Ask the man behind the desk about it. And when he rolls his eyes and looks at you as though you've just escaped from St. Elizabeths mental hospital across the river, remind him that technically, *he* works for *you*. That always works with government employees.

FREER GALLERY OF ART

E. J. Applewhite, in his meticulous and indispensable guide *Washington Itself,* calls the Freer "a haven of exquisiteness, a treasure house of somber wit." It's impossible to put it better. Oscar Wilde would be utterly at home here.

The Freer was built in the 1920s to house Charles Freer's collection of Near and Far Eastern art. Mr.

Applewhite notes, "When you visit the Freer, it helps if you have some familiarity with the vocabulary of calligraphy or the symbolism of Oriental philosophy and religion or even the relation of art to class structure. . . . It is an art for connoisseurs." I don't know about your familiarity with the vocabulary of calligraphy, but mine could use a little brushing up. But it's Whistler's Peacock Room that would have drawn Oscar Wilde.

Wilde and James McNeill Whistler were, as you already well know, friendly adversaries in the orchidaceous London salons of the late nineteenth century. These lushly upholstered rooms were the Algonquin Roundtables of their day, where everyone vied fiercely with one another to say something more clever. Wilde was the greatest conversationalist the English language has ever had, but Whistler could wield his tongue almost as well as he did his brush. Once, after he had said something especially clever, Wilde remarked, "I wish I had said that!" to which Whistler wittily replied, "You will, Oscar, you will." Two points to the gentleman from Lowell, Mass.

Freer qualified for his spot on the Mall by amassing a fortune in railroad car manufacturing. He befriended Whistler in London and proceeded to buy practically everything he painted. But we'll concentrate on this amazing Peacock Room, wherein raged one of the great battles between a temperamental artist and his patron. It stands as a validation of the eternal truth: never leave town while the painter is working on your house. And get the estimate in writing.

In 1876, Whistler was hired by a Liverpool shipowner named Frederick Leyland to paint his London dining room. The room had been designed by an interior architect named Thomas Jeckyll. Jeckyll consulted Whistler on the color scheme for the shutters and doors. Whistler saw his opening and was through it like a shot. Leyland went off to Liverpool to amass more money in hopes of someday being on the American Mall. Whistler meanwhile was having himself a grand old time with the room. By the time he was finished with it, it looked like Aubrey Beardsley and the whole Yellow Book gang had dropped acid and spent the weekend in Mr. Leyland's dining room having a paint-in *à la japonais.* Not only did Whistler repaint every square inch, but he added four enormous peacocks. And you thought *your* painter screwed up?

Needless to say, Mr. Leyland was a wee bit surprised to read about all this, secondhand, in the London papers. Whistler had been writing him letters saying, Everything's going fine, stay in Liverpool, go on with the shipowning gig. In the meantime, he was holding open house to his chums in the media and art world, showing off his latest triumph-in-progress.

Mr. Leyland did what rich people tend to do when they feel they have been taken advantage of: he told Whistler to go stuff his peacocks and ordered up a couple of gallons of Colonial White from Sherwin-Williams.

I'm exaggerating that last part, but he did refuse to pay Whistler his 2,000 guineas. Eventually, he agreed to pay half that, but—rather coolly—wrote Whistler a check for

1,000 pounds, instead of 1,000 guineas. A pound was 20 shillings; a guinea, 21; tradesmen were paid in pounds, artists in guineas.

Whistler did what temperamental artists tend to do when they are dissed by rich patrons: he painted over Leyland's incredibly expensive leather wall hangings with Prussian blue paint and added two more peacocks for good measure. If only world wars were fought this way, the world would be safer and much more interesting to look at.

Not just any two peacocks, mind, but *fighting* pea-cocks, going at it tooth and claw. One had silver feathers resembling the kind of ruffled shirts Leyland favored; the other had a silver crest feather that looked like Whistler's lock of white hair. You didn't need a Ph.D. in art history to figure it out.

To his credit, Leyland did not call in Sherwin-Williams. Freer eventually bought the whole thing and moved it to Detroit. Now it's here, all for you. If you're planning to redecorate, this is the place to come and offer up your (futile) prayers.

Having approximately zero knowledge of "the vocab-ulary of calligraphy" and the other whoosis, here I would ordinarily slink off to Independence Avenue to suck on a hot dog and engage in brutish banter with my fellow proles. But adjoining the Peacock Room are two rooms devoted to American Art, and you should tarry here a moment or two in front of the four-paneled screen entitled *The Four Sylvan Sounds.*

This was done in 1896–97 by Thomas Wilmer Dewing. Its theme is *synesthesia,* a word almost as hard to pronounce as it is to spell, meaning "the stimulation of one sense to produce a secondary effect on another." The paintings are done in ethereal, vibrant shades of sylvan green that draw you in and cast an instant spell. According to the exhibit description, the panels are meant to personify "the wind in the pines, the tap of the woodpecker, the rush of running water, and the song of the hermit thrush." The description alone produces a hypnotic effect. When I snap my fingers, you will awake and buy 10 more copies of this book.

This is, as you already have guessed, an example of the Art for Art's Sake movement championed by Walter Pater—Oscar Wilde's mentor—Whistler, and, most prominently, Wilde. John Ruskin, the formidable British writer and advocate of Gothic naturalism, *detested* the idea of art for art's sake, feeling there was something faintly wanky to it. Reviewing Whistler's painting *Nocturne in Black and Gold,* a night view of a bridge, Ruskin wrote that Whistler was engaged in flinging "a pot of paint in the public's face." God only knows what he would have made of *Overpriced Ink Blot* #7.

A man who could redecorate a billionaire's dining room without permission would hardly take this lying down. Whistler sued Ruskin for defamation. It became a celebrated case. In the end, the court ruled that Ruskin had libeled Whistler, but that he hadn't impaired his ability to make a living, and awarded him damages of—one farthing. The case broke him, emotionally and financially. Whistler repaired to Venice for a year or so and worked on etchings; then he came back to London, gained overdue acclaim, got married, and was happy; but his wife died and that really shattered him, so he traveled, got sick in Holland in 1902, and died in Chelsea soon after. Sorry, didn't mean to rain on your synesthesia.

Now let's exit by the main entrance and cross the Mall northeast in an orderly and diagonal fashion, taking care not to knock over any Frisbee players or demonstrators.

If you have followed instructions carefully, you should now be standing by the back of a building that looks as though it might house a stuffed African elephant, a giant squid, and the world's largest deep-blue diamond. If they don't let you in the back, tell them you are a personal friend of the president. No, better not. Jokes like that don't cause quite the same hilarity as they used to. Just go around to the front.

As you go in, you'll see an old plaque designating this as the National Museum of Natural History and National Museum of Man. Naturally, we don't call it that anymore; it's now known as . . .

NATIONAL MUSEUM OF NATURAL HISTORY

If you have arrived in town with young children, or with a bored teenage daughter, you've come to the right place. The children will be delighted by the dinosaurs, and the teenage daughter will like, omigod, totally think the

Hope Diamond is cool. There is also an IMAX—stands for I Make the Audience Cross-Eyed—theater that will probably be showing a spectacular 360-degree, interactive immersion cinema about—sharks. Sharks have become the Stephen King of the animal kingdom: reliable mass-market willies-instillers. Surf the TV channel late at night and you're guaranteed to come across a rerun of *Jaws: The Revenge,* or a documentary showing a great white gnawing the paint off the bars of a shark cage while someone in scuba gear emits more bubbles than Guy Lombardo on New Year's Eve, or an ad for a $19.95 video called *When Animals Attack!,* showing a great white snarfing down a couple of slow-to-take-off 50-pound pelicans. Whenever I'm tempted to boast about American civilization, this video gives me pause. I came by the museum some years ago and the entire place had been turned over to sharks under the pretext that they're the endangered species. I have little sympathy with that premise. I was attacked by one—a seven-foot-long blue—when I was eight years old and I still twitch whenever I lower myself into a bathtub, so there's nothing more I want to know about them, thanks all the same, other than where to buy one of those bang sticks that delivers a 12-gauge slug directly into their endangered brain stems.

Here we are in another rotunda. But it's a fun one, echoing with jungle sounds, and how about that elephant? Amazingly, Theodore Roosevelt did not shoot it. (Our first conservationist president did, however, bag the ones at the Museum of Natural History in New York.) This is something that U.S. presidents no longer do. Sometimes they'll sneak off and shoot a duck or quail in the company of someone who's donated $30 million to the party. Invariably, this results in a spokesman from People for the Ethical Treatment of Ducks to mist Larry King with spittle the next night. Imagine the White House press secretary declaring that the president is going to Africa to shoot some big game. *As you know, Helen, the president has long wanted to get himself a nice set of ivory tusks for the billiard room at Camp David. He's also hoping to shoot a leopard.* I'd give a year's salary.

Unless paleontology is your bag, or you're with children, you might want to move efficiently through "Life in the Ancient Seas" (wet and terrifying) and even "The World's Largest Invertebrate" (thoroughly revolting). This would be the squid that, I have to say, almost made me bring up my lunchtime chicken wrap. On the day I visited, a group of Japanese tourists were posing for photos in front of a 10,000-year-old woolly mammoth (order *Proboscidea*). Tokyo must be one nonstop slide show. Anyway, the Neanderthal burial diorama was touching: they were among the earliest of our ancestors to bury their dead in bearskins with tools, food, flowers, deer antlers, and baseball mitts; and probably the first to produce grave-robbers. I was impressed by the skull of the 25-foot-long Mososaur that 80 million years ago swam above the Kansas plain "like eels," and keenly grateful not to have been around to witness the spectacle firsthand. By now I was ready for the main event. The Hope Diamond springs eternal.

Jeweler Harry Winston presented it to the Smithsonian in 1958. What's more, he sent it down from New York by U.S. mail. The postage and insurance was $145.29. Tempted as I am, I stopped making jokes about the U.S. mail after a couple of our local mail workers were killed by anthrax.

The world's most famous rock first appeared in 1668 in the hands of a Frenchman named Tavernier. The French, God love 'em, always get there first. It weighed more than 112 carats. He sold it to Louis XIV. Louis had it cut down to 67 carats and turned it into a pendant as part of the crown jewels. Surprisingly, it disappeared during the Revolution, and I'll bet you a large Evian water that it spent some time in the gastrointestinal tract of an enterprising former palace staffer. In 1812, it resurfaced—burp—in London, 20 carats lighter, and was sold to George IV. He died in 1830 and it was bought by the eponymous Henry Philip Hope. In 1912, just about the time that Kate Winslet was preparing to leap off the stern of the *Titanic* with that "Heart of the Ocean" millstone of a diamond around her lovely neck, it arrived in America with Evalyn Walsh McLean. She used to hide it in her cushions and said that it was once worn by her Great Dane, Mike. (At some point, we really must discuss why we don't guillotine our rich people.) At any rate, Harry Winston bought it in 1949 and, mensch that he was, eventually gave it to us. And here it is, 45.52 carats, less than half its original size, flawless, deep blue, surrounded by 16 white diamonds plus a platinum chain bearing 46 more diamonds, and half the population of Tokyo, camera shutters rat-a-tat-tat.

There are other stunning jewels here: earrings that Marie Antoinette had when the pursuers caught up that night at Varennes; the Rosser Reeves star ruby; the 168-carat Mackay Emerald, the size of a charcoal briquette, which only could have been worn by a prima donna of the Metropolitan Opera; and—Good Lord—the 858-carat Gachala Emerald.

As you leave, you might stick your head in the "Birds of D.C." exhibit, but after all this gemological opulence, the cedar waxwing and tufted titmouse might be a bit of a letdown, despite their abundant charms. On the other hand, *Even Solomon in all his glory was not arrayed like one of these.* Right?

As you walk out the Constitution Avenue entrance and turn left toward the next big building, visualize for a moment the canal that once ran where the avenue now is. Now imagine the rotting carcasses, mosquitoes, outbreaks of Yellow Fever. You were saying about the "good old days"?

When you come to the building with a large Möbius-strip sculpture outside, go in.

The National Museum of American History

This is where the Smithsonian earns the "nation's attic" title. There's enough here, from the original star-spangled banner that flew over Fort McHenry to Archie Bunker's chair, to keep all tastes engaged for hours.

I was once here with my wife and children, for a publication party for a book written by Lynne Cheney, wife of Vice President Richard Cheney. It's a delightful and nicely illustrated book called *America—A Patriotic Primer*. As Mrs. Cheney spoke, dozens of toddlers crawled about the stage. We began with the Pledge of Allegiance. This was just before the Ninth U.S. Circuit Court banned the Pledge in California and other western state schools on the grounds that the "under God" clause made it unconstitutional. All I can say is, it felt great to say the Pledge that night, even to the sound of the wall separating church and state crashing down around our feet.

In her remarks, Mrs. Cheney reminded everyone that Washington had been described (by Robert E. Lee's father) this way: "First in war, first in peace, first in the hearts of his countrymen." She had us all repeat the quote out loud and that felt great, too. A Republican Romper Room. I like Mrs. Cheney. She has a Ph. D.-sharp mind in the package of a lovable grade school teacher. As a surprise she produced an actual vice president of the United States, not that this terribly impressed the two-year-olds onstage. After this, we were turned loose on the museum, which had been transformed into a "patriotic picnic" featuring hamburgers, hot dogs, pizza, fried chicken, popcorn, ice cream, along with booths where you could learn to fold the U.S. flag into a tight triangle, sign your own copy of the Declaration of Independence with a quill pen, or make a Lincoln stovepipe hat, all to the accompaniment of an oom-pah-pah band dressed in red stripes and boater hats. I don't think I've ever had a "more fun-ner" time—as my 10-year-old son Conor put it—in Washington.

But no evening with kids can truly be fun unless you embarrass them. So I made them wait outside the "American Presidency" exhibit on the third floor while the Cheneys progressed through it. You can generally tell if a vice president is about to appear, because he will be preceded through the door by four or five Secret Service agents ready to wrestle you to the ground if necessary, three or four staffers, and a photographer.

"Mr. Vice President!" I shrieked. This immediately induced deep mortification in my children. But sports that they are, he and Mrs. Cheney came over and shook hands all around. My children have still not forgiven me for my appalling lack of decorum, but I suspect it made lifelong Republicans of them, and that was my goal.

Once the Cheneys had vacated the "American Presidency" exhibit, it was no longer, in the dismal phrase of the Secret Service, a "sterile area," and we could enter. Such crown jewels as we have in America are here. That may strike you as a grandiose sentiment as you contemplate a 1960 shopping bag proclaiming, "HOUSEWIVES FOR NIXON-LODGE. A GREAT TEAM!" or another item identified as an authentic "Decorated Styrofoam hat worn by a New Mexico delegate to the 1988 Atlanta Democratic Convention," to say nothing of the "Papier-mâché pineapple hat worn by a Robert Dole supporter from the Ohio delegation at the 1996 San Diego Republican Convention," but trust me, it gets better.

Moments later, you're standing silently in front of a case displaying George Washington's general officer's uniform from the 1790s. He might well have been wearing this when he surveyed the land you're standing on. Washington was six-foot-three—his biographer Richard Brookhiser notes that the average height of one of his soldiers was five-foot-eight—and he hasn't shrunk an inch since. He was also, to judge from the elegant waist, gym-trim. It's tempting to ascribe this leanness to those appetite-diminishing hippopotamus dentures, but more likely it was due to the discipline he evinced in every other aspect of his life, most significantly for us, in his refusal to be turned into king, president-for-life, and even god.

To the right of the uniform is a small scarlet leather chest in which he kept the papers from the Constitutional Convention in 1787. It is in the shape, appropriately, of a treasure chest. Another object to give awestruck pause is the small mahogany lap desk on which Thomas Jefferson wrote the document that ends with the sentence, "And for the support of this declaration, with a firm reliance on the protection of Divine Providence, we mutually pledge to each other our lives, our fortunes, and our sacred honor."

Over here is the carriage that Ulysses S. Grant rode in to his second inauguration. And here's Laura Bush's ruby-red inaugural gown and the "football" briefcase that contained the nuclear launch codes carried by President Clinton's military aide. It's a challenge explaining to a 10-year-old the concept of a briefcase that could end life on planet Earth. *Do not try this at home.* Franklin Roosevelt's cape that he wore at Yalta, Ike's summer uniform, Andrew Jackson's sword from the War of 1812.

Here's a TV monitor showing Richard Nixon, surely our most awkward president, relaxing, walking on the beach at San Clemente in his black suit and polished black dress shoes. One can only shake one's head and mutter, for the thousandth time, *Du-de!* Meanwhile, here are some ashtrays from *Air Force One.*

Air Force One amenity items have always been in hot demand. We used to fly on it whenever Mr. Bush was dispatched to represent the president at a significant foreign funeral. His motto was, "You die, I fly." At Andrews Air Force Base, there would be a race up the gangway to get aboard first so that you could scoop up stationery pads, playing cards, and cigarettes embossed with the presidential seal. This would take care of the Christmas shopping for that year.

If this appalls you, you're quite right, but we weren't the only ones who craved *Air Force One* tchotchkes. John Ehrlichman, Nixon's close aide, recounts the story in his wonderfully bitchy memoir, *Witness to Power: The Nixon Years,* of arriving at his White House office on his first day on the job and taking a panicked call from the young military aide who had accompanied ex–President Lyndon Johnson home to Texas aboard *Air Force One.*

"They're taking everything!" the aide whispered frantically.

"What do you mean, everything?" said Ehrlichman.

"I mean, they're *stripping the plane.*" LBJ wanted it all for his presidential library. He ordered them to remove the furnishings, carpet, even the toilet paper.

This presented Ehrlichman with his first dilemma as White House counselor. He wisely instructed the aide to let them take it all. Sometimes you've just got to let it go. If only Mr. Ehrlichman's subsequent decisions had been as sage.

You can meditate on that while you're standing in front of the file cabinet that once belonged to Daniel Ellsberg's psychiatrist, Dr. Lewis Fielding. Ellsberg had leaked the top secret "Pentagon Papers" to the media, prompting the Nixon White House to assemble a group of ex–CIA and FBI men called "the Plumbers" to plug leaks and find out what Ellsberg had told his shrink. (One wonders if Dr. Fielding said to his patient after the burglary, "And how did it make you feel?") James Bond, these people were not. It looks as though they attacked it with sledgehammer and crowbar, or maybe even a bulldozer. These nimble cat burglars went on to fame in an office building in town called the Watergate.

On a more uplifting note, here's astronaut Alan Shepard's space suit, and here a plaster cast of Abraham Lincoln's hands. The caption notes that "Lincoln's right hand was still swollen from shaking hands with congratulating supporters." On New Year's Day 1907, President

Theodore Roosevelt shook the hands of 8,100 callers at the White House. Goes with the job, but Roosevelt had become president because his predecessor had been shot in a reception line. Me, I'd have been a bit wary. Perhaps he felt protected by the talisman he wore. Edmund Morris, his biographer, notes in *Theodore Rex* that he wore a "strange, heavy gold ring on his left third finger" that contained a strand of Lincoln's hair, a ring given to him by Secretary of State John Hay, a former aide to Lincoln.

Speaking of TR, here are two remarkable items: the speech text and eyeglasses case that stopped an assassin's bullet from mortally penetrating his chest in Milwaukee on October 14, 1912, while he was campaigning for a third term as the Bull Moose candidate. The speech text ran to 50 pages, and it's good thing, too, because a shorter speech might not have stopped the slug. Despite oozing blood from the chest, Roosevelt insisted on delivering the speech. The newspaper account of his performance is both heroic and hilarious. Shoot a Republican president in the chest and he'll manage to find the humor in it. On March 30, 1981, as President Reagan was being wheeled into surgery, he looked up at the doctors and said, "Please tell me you're all Republicans."

There's no humor to be mined in the exhibit about the murder of another Republican. The sign says, "One of the Smithsonian's most treasured icons is this top hat, worn by Lincoln to Ford's Theater on the night of his assassination." Here, too, is the bloodstained shirt cuff of Laura Keene, the star of *Our American Cousin,* who, according to legend, cradled Lincoln's head. (Perhaps dubious, as we'll see later on.) We'll visit Ford's Theater and see the other heartbreaking artifacts, so there's no need to dwell more here. But here's the "Induction Balance" machine device, a kind of early sonogram, that Alexander Graham Bell used in July and August of 1881 to try to locate the bullets inside the dying President Garfield. Here, too, are President Clinton's saxophone, Harry Truman's loud Key West shirt, and Grover Cleveland's trout flies. And Ike's golf clubs. In the 1950s, Ike was accused by the Nutball Right of being a communist. Conservative philosopher Russell Kirk put that to rest with his quip, "Eisenhower isn't a communist; he's a golfer."

I've left out a lot, but I do want to point out the collection of locks of hair from Washington, Adams, Jefferson, Madison, Monroe, John Quincy Adams, Jackson, Van Buren, Harrison, Tyler, Polk, Taylor, Fillmore, and Pierce. Obviously, someone back then heard a voice whispering, *Collect them all!* As soon as we get the cloning thing down, we can stop bothering with presidential elections and design our future leaders from among this abundance of hirsute DNA.

There's much else to explore here, but I'll let you poke about the museum on your own. I do, however, urge you to check out the famously dweadful statue of George Washington. You cannot miss it. They literally built this museum around it. When it was first installed in the Capitol Rotunda in 1841, they had to remove the marble doors and some of the masonry to get it in. It was so heavy that it began to go through the Aquia Creek sandstone. Finally they moved it outside, where for a half-century it served as a Olympian birdbath for the capital's pigeon population. When it was being carted by 22 herniating oxen from Florence, Italy, to the coast to be put aboard a U.S. Navy man-o-war, the locals along the way thought it was a statue of a saint and fell to the ground, crossing themselves. All this ignominy brought little joy to its sculptor, Horatio Greenough, who had labored for eight years to produce his marble apotheosis, but then no one specifically *asked* him to portray our unassuming Founding Father as Zeus, naked from the waist up, in a posture so ridiculously heroic that one teenage boy I observed studying it was moved to remark to his schoolmate, "Who's the dick?" Washington is not specifically remembered for his sense of humor, but I somehow feel that he'd understand.

No, on second thought, I don't think he would.

Walk Two

Washington Monument

M oving from the profane to the sacred, let's head over to the Washington Monument. I won't bother telling you how to find it. It's the only 555-foot-high obelisk in town.

After it was finally completed in 1884, it was the tallest structure in the world for five years, until the French decided this was an intolerable affront to their national pride and instructed M. Eiffel to put up something even bigger. But our *objet* is still the largest freestanding piece of masonry in the world. It's appropriate that the cornerstone was laid on July 4, 1848, by a Mr. B. B. French, Grand Master of Masons, and that he wore the same Masonic apron Washington wore and used the same trowel when he well and truly laid the Capitol cornerstone in 1793.

Work on the monument had long since ground to a halt when Mark Twain set eyes on it in the 1870s. "It has the aspect," he wrote in *The Gilded Age,* "of a factory chimney with the top broken off. The skeleton of a decaying scaffolding lingers about its summit, and tradition says that the spirit of Washington often comes down and sits on those rafters to enjoy this tribute of respect which the nation has reared as the symbol of its unappeasable gratitude."

Twain was only just warming up. "The Monument is to be finished, some day," he continued, "and at that time our Washington will have risen still higher in the nation's veneration, and will be known as the Great-Great-Grandfather of his Country. The memorial Chimney stands in a quiet pastoral locality that is full of reposeful expression. With a glass you can see the cow-sheds about its base, and the contented sheep nibbling pebbles in the desert solitudes that surround it, and the tired pigs dozing in the holy calm of its protecting shadow."

Putting up monuments on the Mall is always a process of tiptoeing through a minefield while carrying blocks of marble, but it does seem odd that it took 85 years to put up something to the man who bequeathed us our country. But then it's probably his fault in the first place, for passing on the equestrian statue L'Enfant wanted to erect.

The saga has its pathetic, even appalling, moments: when the Washington National Monument Society finally embarked in the 1830s to raise the $1 million to build Robert Mills's design, they came up with a total of $30,000, much of it from one-dollar donations. By 1855 they had raised a total of $230,339.40. (About $4,600,000 today.)

Then, in 1854, when Pope Pius IX donated a stone, as leaders of other countries were doing, a Baltimore preacher named Weishample gave a fiery-mad sermon urging good American Protestants to reject this block of satanic marble. (Which had been taken, as it happens, from Rome's Temple of Concord.) A posse of masked men belonging to the Know Nothing Party attacked the guard and made off with the fiendish "Pope Stone," smashing it and dumping it into the Potomac, where it still lies amid the silt, waiting until the Antichrist shall rise.

Surprisingly, this had a dampening effect on further donations of stone. Then the Civil War came along and suddenly it made more sense to build forts than giant ceno-taphs to dead founders, however venerable. It wasn't until the Centennial in 1876 that a collective sense of *This is get-ting to be kind of embarrassing* prompted the government to turn to the agency of last resort, the good old U.S. Army Corps of Engineers. The U.S. Minister in Rome researched the classical dimensions of an obelisk and produced a for-mula for its size (height equals 10 times the base), and the diligent Lieutenant Colonel Thomas Casey took it from there. Above the capstone, a 3,300-pound hunk of rock, is an aluminum pyramid weighing 100 ounces studded with 144 platinum-tipped lightning conductors. This was low-ered into place on December 6, 1884, in a raging gale. When the rare pyramid of aluminum was exhibited in New

York City and Washington, visitors asked to step over it so that they could say they had stepped over the top of the tallest building in the world. My copy of *Keim's Illustrated Hand-book of Washington and Its Environs,* printed one year later, notes that it cost $225 (about $4,000 today) and "is the largest block of Aluminium ever made." It was inscribed with the names of those who worked on the Monument. The east face is inscribed with the words, "Laus Deo" (Praise to God). The Ninth Circuit ought really to do something about this.

At any rate, 1884 was a good year, giving us, in addition to the Monument, *The Adventures of Huckleberry Finn,* cocaine as a local anesthetic, the Waterman pen, the Louisville Slugger baseball bat, the Dakota apartment building in New York City, and Quaker Oats in a can, one of the first packaged foods. And 30 years after the evil Pope Stone had been heaved into the Potomac, a phrase that had attached itself to the Republican candidate James G. Blaine, calling the Democrats the party of "Rum, Romanism and Rebellion," happily proved politically incorrect.

I'll wait outside while you go up the Monument. I climbed every one of those 898 steps one day in 1965 and my knees haven't been right since. (Not that they let you climb up anymore—you might stop to release anthrax spores on the people below you.)

On the other hand, you shouldn't feel that you *have* to go inside. It's a bit of a hassle now, what with having to show up first thing to get tickets, and of course now the metal detectors and all the rest. It's far more dramatic viewed from the outside anyway, and the view from up there is no improvement over that from the window of the U.S. Airways shuttle to New York.

While I was working at the White House, one day a man backed a van up to the base of the Monument. He announced that it was packed with dynamite. The Monument is a half-mile away, but the Secret Service calculated that the "blast radius" would be enough to blow out our windows, so we got the day off. A police sharpshooter eventually killed this troubled soul, and it turned out there wasn't much in his van but dirty laundry. A few years before, an undermedicated army helicopter pilot crashed into the White House. And a few years after that, someone opened fire on the White House from the sidewalk, causing the eventual closing off of Pennsylvania Avenue to traffic. And then a few years after that on a beautiful September morning, a plane flew into the Pentagon. Things seem to be escalating.

I'll just point out the small block of stone slightly west and north of the Monument's base: this marks the spot where L'Enfant's original north-south and east-west axes intersected, and where George's equestrian statue was to prance. When they got around to the Monument, they realized that the ground beneath would not support an 81,120-ton obelisk. It would hardly do to have a Leaning Washington Monument. (Too Italian.) At any rate, this way our presidents have a clear view from the Blue Room of the White House to the Jefferson Memorial.

A parting thought: there used to be a glorious view from here over the Reflecting Pool to the Lincoln Memorial. No longer. This once pulse-quickening vista is now interrupted by a memorial to World War II. This was authorized by the House and Senate, with curious haste, in 2001. With all respect to the Greatest Generation, it is ironic, even inexplicable, that in their rush to throw up a memorial to World War II (57 years later), that they erected something that looks as though it had been designed by Albert Speer, architect of the Third Reich. But there it is, a reminder of the continuing cost of the nation's unappeasable gratitude. Well, every monument on the Mall has begun by being hated; perhaps in time we will learn to love this one.

If you walk east to 15th Street and turn south, the street turns into Raoul Wallenberg Place. This gives you an idea where we're headed. Wallenberg was the Swedish diplomat who during World War II saved thousands of Budapest Jews, only to be executed, it now appears, by the Soviets after the war in the Lubyanka, the KGB prison in Moscow.

Over the entrance to his inferno, Dante hung a sign saying, "Abandon Hope, All Ye Who Enter Here." The Nazis put up signs over the gates to theirs that said, *Arbeit Macht Frei,* "Work Will Make You Free."

UNITED STATES
HOLOCAUST MEMORIAL MUSEUM

Etched into the stone near the entrance of the Holocaust Museum are the following words, uttered by Eisenhower on April 15, 1945: "The things I saw beggar
description. . . ."

When the project was begun in the late 1980s, some,
including myself, wondered, Why here? Surely Berlin or
Munich would be a more apt pedestal for a Holocaust
memorial?

I put off coming here until I had seen the ultimate
memorial to the Holocaust outside Cracow in Poland—
Auschwitz. Having now seen the Holocaust Memorial in
Washington, I'm glad that it's here. Not so much for the
manner in which it curates one of the worst chapters in
human history as for its emotional impact, which I watched
play out on a group of teenagers from the Midwest. They
went in noisy and came out quiet.

As you step off the elevator to start the exhibit on the
top floor, you hear the words over speakers: "A report
came over the radio and it said, 'We've found something
and we don't know what it is.' "

In front of you is a photograph of GIs at Ohrdruf
concentration camp standing over a pile of partially cre-
mated Jews. By this point, these weary young men had
fought their way across Europe. They had witnessed every
horror there was, and yet here, at the end of their long
ordeal, was something that even they could not have

imagined. So the memorial begins through American eyes, validating its place here.

Nothing I point out will be new, but the facts bear endless reiteration, beginning with this one: In 1933, there were nine million Jews in Europe. By 1945, two out of three had been murdered. You could leave it at that. But here is photograph, life-size, of a Brown Shirt holding a muzzled German shepherd. The shepherd is impatient to savage the observer. It's a terrifying photo, and this is what they saw. Here's another, of teenage blond girls in braided pigtails, giving the Nazi salute; of Hitler putting his hands on the shoulder of a youth in a creepy, quasi-fatherly way. Here's a Hollerith machine, one of the first computers of its day, with an accompanying quotation by one Willy Heidinger: "We are proud to be able to contribute to such a task . . . so that our physician [Hitler] can determine whether, from the standpoint of the nation's health, the computed data correlates in a harmonious, that is, healthy, relationship—or whether diseased conditions must be cured by corrective interventions." The Hollerith machine was used by the SS to keep track of how many Jews had been shipped off to be gassed. Over here we see Einstein and Freud emigrating (separately) following Kristallnacht in 1938. The two most consequential men of their day—of their age!—and the Nazis drove them out. Over here is a photo of a doctor, smiling over the corpse of a retarded child who has just been killed. At some point in this display you begin to wonder what impulse led the Nazis to be such thorough documentarians of their own monstrosities. A friend of mine, a distinguished British historian, was once shown the film taken of the execution by meat hook and piano wire of the October plotters. Were they planning to show it in newsreels after they'd won the war?

On the next floor down, hidden from children's eyes, are looped videos of photo stills showing mobile death squad atrocities committed by Lithuanian nationalists, beating to death 50 Jews with iron bars, reviving them with water, then starting in again, finally posing over the swollen bodies like weekend hunters. Afterward, they sang the Lithuanian national anthem.

You walk through one of the actual rail cars that transported them to the camps. This one went to Treblinka. You stand in it and imagine them suffocating or freezing on the three- or four-day ride to being gassed. Go down the hall and there's a photo of the hair at Auschwitz. I saw the real thing: a room containing two tons of human hair shorn from the victims after being murdered. This pile was the remnant that hadn't been turned into felt slippers, boat bumpers, and mattress stuffing. At Auschwitz I was told that they were going to send some of it to the Washington memorial, but in the end it was decided it would be "too much."

The U.S. Holocaust Memorial releases you back into the present through a Hall of Remembrance, where a flame burns and Deuteronomy warns: "Only guard yourself and guard your soul carefully, lest you forget the things your eyes saw . . ."

Take a left down Raoul Wallenberg Place and you will shortly arrive at the . . .

Bureau of Engraving and Printing (U.S. Mint)

This is, as Willie Sutton would say, "Where the money is." It is also Uncle Sam as Big Brother. It escapes me why being admitted to this building, where you walk along a narrow catwalk and look through bullet-proof plate glass at stacks of freshly printed one dollar bills worth $320,000, should require going through more security hoops than boarding *Air Force One*. Are they really expecting us to produce jackhammers, break through the glass, and leap down and start stuffing our pockets with giant sheets of specie? The final affront came when we were sternly admonished to tie our shoelaces before ascending an escalator. A wonder they didn't confiscate them. This came after being growled at not to touch the ceiling lest we all be immediately "removed." I do understand the need to go through metal detectors these days, and am eager to play my part, but honestly. If I were you, I'd take a pass on this, the most tourist-unfriendly site in Washington, and head directly for the Jefferson Memorial. But here is what I learned at the Mint: a one dollar bill lasts a year and a half. A one hundred dollar bill lasts nine years, depending on how many times it gets rolled up and used to snort coke.

JEFFERSON MEMORIAL

You can't miss the Jefferson Memorial so I won't harass you with directions. But first you'll have to go retrieve your small shoulder bag from the tree where you hid it, because the Praetorian Guard at the Bureau of Engraving and Printing declared it technically "not a woman's purse" and therefore likely to contain a homemade nuclear device.

As I walked along the rim of the Tidal Basin, I couldn't help wondering, for the umpteenth time, where it was precisely along this neat littoral back in 1974 that Congressman Wilbur Mills of Arkansas and his enamorata stripper, Fanne Foxe ("The Argentine Firecracker"), came to grief with the D.C. police. You'll recall that while the congressman was explaining his eminence along with the booze on his breath to the officers, Ms. Foxe made matters worse by leaping into the Tidal Basin. What *is* it with politicians from Arkansas? I rebuked myself for approaching Jefferson's temple with these lurid meditations.

Walking up its steps made me feel, once again, like a Roman come to pay his respects to the god. I saw a pleasant-looking young park ranger and inquired if there was a tour today. He said, "Would you *like* a tour?" Well, yes, I said, if it's not too much trouble. "You bet," he grinned enthusiastically and for the next hour I found myself in the able hands of Ranger Michael T. Kelly, as engaging and knowledgeable and passionate a guide as I have ever encountered in the city. The park rangers rotate from one site to another to stave off boredom, so it was my good fortune to have Ranger Mike that day.

We stood on the steps facing north toward the White House. The reason you can see the White House so clearly from here—and vice versa—is that President Franklin Roosevelt, to whom we owe the Jefferson Memorial, ordered all the trees blocking his view to be chopped down so that he could keep an eye on the progress. Imagine trying that today. And those weren't the only trees that died for the Jefferson. The famous cherry trees that line the Tidal Basin, causing traffic jams every spring, presented the Jefferson's builders with a delicate challenge in 1938.

"The idea of disturbing the cherry trees was blasphemy," explained Ranger Mike, "so these prominent ladies of Washington came down and chained themselves to the trees." FDR's secretary of the interior Harold Ickes came up with a simple yet elegant solution: he sent the ladies tea and coffee. When they could no longer "postpone the inevitable" (rangers do not make direct allusions to having to go to the bathroom), "Bam—that's when they cut them down." If it had been a few years later, in the days following Pearl Harbor, those ladies might have helped the workmen chop down the trees. These had been the gift of the City of Tokyo back in 1912, partly as a gesture of thanks for our part in ending the Russo-Japanese War. After December 7, 1941, some impetuous citizens vented their fury on the poor trees. Guards had to be posted.

When President Roosevelt arrived to dedicate the memorial on April 13, 1943, the bicentennial of Jefferson's birth, the crowd never caught so much as a glimpse of his wheelchair. FDR preferred to keep his disability from the public view. The press was actually forbidden to photograph him in it. When we get to the new FDR Memorial next door, it may come as a shock to find a statue of the president sitting by himself in a plaza in a pose that seems calculated to emphasize his infirmity. There was a fierce battle over this between the disabled lobby and the historical purists who wanted to respect FDR's wishes. The latter lost. But back to Jefferson, and to the city he had in mind back in 1791.

Here on the steps of his temple is the perfect vantage point from which to trace the original shoreline of the Federal City, roughly from the Bureau of Engraving and Printing to that little stone marker northwest of the Washington Monument. Everything between you and that line was Potomac River. You see how extensive is the landfill. You can also see from here the whole of L'Enfant's plan—and Jefferson's plan. They were quite distinct.

Jefferson befriended L'Enfant and provided him with maps of European capitals from his extensive library. But like everyone in Washington since—*he had an agenda!* (It was when I came to Washington that I first learned that the word *agenda* was synonymous with "sinister intentions.") Jefferson, ever the agrarian, did not want the Federal City to evolve into a huge, bustling metropolis. To that end, he wanted to put the Congress House right about where the State Department now is, near 21st Street. The President's Palace, he wanted to put atop a hill

just west of that, in the little German settlement called
Hamburg. That would have scrunched the city into a very
small area. Worse, if Jefferson had had his way, we might
today be calling the White House "Hamburger Hill."

Jefferson's collaboration with L'Enfant produced a city
laid out on a rational grid, but with L'Enfant's trademark
radial axes of avenues diagonally crisscrossing the city.
L'Enfant's idea was that the various states would adopt
the 15 city squares and develop them, putting up their own
obelisks and statues and such. Thus would the city become
a microcosm of the nation. He wanted to stimulate settlement around these squares, and hoped that this system
might erase the divisions between the southern and northern states. Clever idea, and therefore, of course, doomed
from the start.

No one seems to know who, exactly, named the
avenues after the states. According to an article by Pamela
Scott in the journal of the District of Columbia Historical
Society, it was Jefferson and the commissioners who came
up with the (rather prosaic) idea of naming the streets on
the grid with simple numbers and letters. "Who was defin-
itively responsible for naming the diagonal avenues is
unknown," she notes. "The inherent logic of the names of
the diagonal avenues argues that they were laid out by
L'Enfant with interrelated symbolic, aesthetic, and practical
purposes in mind. Their location within the city reflected
each state's geographic location within the country and they
were clustered around squares intended to contain buildings associated with important revolutionary events that

took place in those states. Their lengths were not a function of the size of the states (*vide* Rhode Island Avenue) but rather the amount and importance of revolutionary activity within each state." This explains why Massachusetts and Pennsylvania Avenues are so prominent, while, say, Idaho remains an avenue in search of greatness.

At any rate, President Washington eventually sided with L'Enfant's plan over Jefferson's, and Congress, of course, sided with Washington. The Congress House went up on Jenkins Hill and we were spared Hamburger Hill. "So I think," Ranger Mike said, "that the city owes as much to Washington as to L'Enfant."

We went inside. A stiff breeze whipped through the colonnades across pink and gray Tennessee marble. The 19-foot-high heroic-scale statue used up so much bronze during the war that its casting was temporarily halted. (Remember what other monument is 19 feet high? That's right: *Freedom,* atop the Capitol.)

Jefferson stands more erect than he did, apparently, in life. According to historian Joseph J. Ellis, Jefferson was a bit of a slouch, literally. He was taller than Washington, but he lacked Washington's military posture. One senator observed, "He sits in a lounging manner on one hip, commonly, and with one of his shoulders elevated much above the other." He would receive diplomats and other eminent guests wearing slippers and ratty corduroy pants. Our first grunge president. And the man who wrote the most stirring document in American history was a terrible public speaker. In eight years as president, he gave exactly two speeches—his inaugurals. He much preferred to put it in writing. But what writing.

"I HAVE SWORN ON THE ALTAR OF GOD, ETERNAL HOSTIL-ITY TO EVERY FORM OF TYRANNY OVER THE MIND OF MAN." The words carved around the base of the dome are always stirring to the blood, never mind all those slaves he owned and, uh, enjoyed. As Richard Brookhiser has pointed out, of the nine presidents who owned slaves, only George Washington freed his upon his death.

Ranger Mike pointed out that Jefferson is not looking out toward the White House, as is generally supposed, but just east of it—at the Treasury Building named for his great rival, Alexander Hamilton. "He's keeping an eye on him." He grinned, "But he could *also* be looking at the site he'd picked out where *his* city would have been laid out."

I thanked Ranger Mike and made my exit in the direction of the memorial to the man who had brought this one about.

FRANKLIN DELANO ROOSEVELT MEMORIAL

I grumbled and groaned when, in the mid-1990s, I saw the fence going up around a seven-and-a-half acre piece of West Potomac Park. That's a big chunk of the Monopoly board. I grew up in a household where FDR was generally referred to as "that man," and Mrs. Roosevelt as "that woman." Didn't the architect of the New Deal already *have* a memorial in Washington? Indeed he did, the "block" the size of his desk that he asked Supreme Court Justice Felix Frankfurter to make sure got put up in front of the National Archives. And now they were plowing up this vast expanse of national turf—"sacred soil is the customary term," as Twain said—for another memorial?

Roosevelt, like another president whose memorial we'll visit shortly, died at a historically propitious moment: his hour of triumph. It was April 12, 1945. (Lincoln died 80 years earlier almost to the day.) Hitler was locked inside his bunker with what was left of his Thousand Year Reich, his mistress, dog, pistol, and cyanide capsules. The war in Europe would be over in three weeks. At Los Alamos in the New Mexico desert, American scientists were preparing to set off an explosion that would end the war with Japan. So the impact of FDR's death, coming when it did, was momentous.

On April 12, 1995, the fiftieth anniversary of FDR's death, the morning newspapers had been full of reminiscences. I boarded the New York-Washington shuttle and saw by chance the mother of a college roommate. It was on her forearm, and on that of her husband, now dead, at a seder in 1972 that I had seen my first concentration camp serial number tattoo. Fifty years ago on this day, Mrs. Edith Dach had been behind barbed wire, starving, wondering if each day would be the last. I asked her, Did she learn that day about Roosevelt's death? Yes, she said, they had. What was the reaction inside the camp? "We thought we would be killed. We thought that now the war would be over, since Roosevelt was dead." I brought this memory with me into the memorial.

It's entirely linear, history as split-level, four "rooms" for each of his terms. It's a fascinating, busy area full of surprises: statue after statue, a wall of Braille and five pillars arranged in a quincunx rubbed shiny, along with waterfalls, plantings, and quotes chiseled into dark granite.

FDR greets us in the first plaza, in his wheelchair. At this distance, with his opaque bronze eyeglasses and upturned hat, he looks like James Joyce sitting on a toilet. President Clinton weighed in on the fracas over whether he should be depicted as disabled. He got Congress to shove through an authorization for the statue. The memorial cost $48 million. Forty-two of that was paid for by the government. The wheelchair statue cost $1.5 and was paid for by the National Organization on Disability.

If I were a Roosevelt, I'd be upset that my famous relative was posthumously hijacked to satisfy a zeitgeist that requires putting your disability front and center. But here it is. I preferred the statue of him with his Scotty dog, Fala. He's wearing the cape that we saw back at the National Museum of American History, and if he's sitting in his wheelchair, you can't see it. There's also a frieze showing him riding in an open car. Ironic that at the moment of maximum danger, our leaders could still go about in open cars. That custom would end soon enough. There's no depiction of him and Mrs. Roosevelt together, though there is a bronze of Eleanor toward the end. The most memorable photographs of FDR don't include Mrs. Roosevelt. He died in the company of his longtime mistress, Lucy Mercer, in Warm Springs, Georgia.

Come here in the evening, when the light is soft and the granite blocks seem less severe and you can listen, between planes roaring by overhead, to the splash of the waterfalls.

Now do a U-turn and head north along the Tidal Basin, taking care not to get run over by Arkansas politicians and strippers. Take a right on West Basin Drive, a left on Independence, and a right on Daniel French Drive. This sounds much more complicated than it is. Stop when you see 19 soldiers on your right.

KOREAN WAR VETERANS MEMORIAL

After the Vietnam Veterans Memorial was built in 1982— and we'll be there in just a moment—the veterans of other wars began to say, "Hey, what about us?" They didn't put it quite like that, but that was the gist. The result was this striking memorial to the Korean conflict, and the monumental, vista-ruining World War II Memorial they are building as I write this.

Once you see the Vietnam Memorial, you'll find that the Korean Memorial is essentially a fusing of its two elements: an engraved black granite wall and statues. The Korean is also best viewed toward twilight—or better still, in the rain or snow, much as I hate to send you out into the elements.

The squad of soldiers is on patrol, their carbines and radio antennae protruding from beneath rain ponchos. There's a weary look on the last soldier, whose head is turned, mouth open in fear. He's just heard something.

Along the long black granite wall are photographic-process etchings of soldiers and the tools of their war. If you come here at just the right time of day, the wall disappears, leaving only the ghostly images. It doesn't quite have the emotional impact of the Vietnam Wall, but it is ingenious and worthy of the men and women who saved Korea. The inscription at the foot of the first soldier in front reads:

> OUR NATION HONORS HER SONS AND DAUGHTERS WHO ANSWERED THE CALL TO DEFEND A COUNTRY THEY NEVER KNEW AND A PEOPLE THEY NEVER MET. 1950—KOREA—1953.

On the far side of the Reflecting Pool you will see people disappearing into the ground as they walk. This is the . . .

VIETNAM VETERANS MEMORIAL

I was here on November 13, 1982, the day it was dedicated. At the periphery of the crowd, I saw a marine, his chest crowded with decorations, in ceremonial dress. He turned away from the Wall and put a white gloved hand to the bridge of his nose, and wept. That moment has stayed with me forever.

One night in 1979, a young veteran of the war named Jan Scruggs who had served in the army as an infantry corporal went to see the movie *The Deer Hunter.* Scruggs had been wounded in the war and decorated for bravery. He came home that night depressed and stayed up all night wondering why there was no memorial to the men and women who had died in Vietnam.

Back in the late 1970s, Vietnam was still a dirty word. The last thing on anyone's mind was a memorial. Against all odds, Scruggs proceeded to get one built.

The story behind the building of the Wall would occupy a book of its own. It turned into a refighting of the war. Scruggs and his comrades persuaded Texas multimillionaire (and eventual presidential candidate) H. Ross Perot to fund a design competition. Perot had been magnificently generous toward Vietnam vets.

As part of their research, members of the design committee paid a visit to Rock Creek Cemetery in Washington. There was a particular grave they wanted to see, that of Marian Hooper Adams. Clover—her nickname—Adams was married to Henry Adams, the grandson of John Quincy Adams and anonymously the author of the great American novel *Democracy.* His other master work is his autobiography, *The Education of Henry Adams.*

Mrs. Adams committed suicide in their house on Lafayette Square in 1885. Adams commissioned the most famous sculptor of the day, Augustus Saint-Gaudens, to do a memorial to his wife. It's all in black, of a woman seated, her head shrouded in a cape. Gaudens said of it, "Some call it the Peace of God, some Nirvana. To me it is the human soul face to face with the greatest of all mysteries." It is usually called, more simply, "Grief." It stops you cold.

In due course, the design submissions came in. Many were heroic. One depicted a soldier waiting for the helicopter to evacuate him, his arms outstretched in a pose of crucifixion.

One submission, from a 21-year-old Asian-American architecture student at Yale named Maya Ying Lin, was minimalist, in keeping with academic vogue. It consisted of two black walls sunken into the ground forming a V. It reminded the jury of "Grief." They voted for Lin's design.

All hell broke loose. A former marine officer named James Webb, one of the most highly decorated soldiers of the war and author of the harrowing Vietnam novel *Fields of Fire,* had been enlisted by Scruggs to serve on the original memorial committee. Webb *hated* the design. One fellow veteran and design contestant called it a "black gash of shame." Ross Perot also hated it and announced that he felt sandbagged. Author Tom Wolfe declared it "a wailing wall for the draft dodgers and New Lefters of the future." It was also called "a tribute to Jane Fonda." The various committees that rule on memorials on the Mall were lobbied furiously to kill it. Somehow, amazingly, Scruggs and his allies got it built. The breakthrough compromise was agreeing to add a heroic statue and flagpole.

The memorial immediately became the most visited site in Washington. If you have ever stood before it and seen the 58,209 names on the two walls, no explanation is needed. If you haven't, no explanation will suffice.

On the south side of the memorial, you'll find the bronze trio of soldiers done by Frederick Hart. They're returning from a patrol and have just heard something in the bush. As someone noted at the time, it catches the faces of "young men at the moment when the shadow of death is passing over them."

When I first saw it, it was still clay, in Rick Hart's studio overlooking the alley down which John Wilkes Booth made his escape. I had come with Jim Webb, Hart's friend and a prime instigator of the idea of adding the statue that had now been in there for two years. In Webb's view, and in that of many other veterans, Hart's statue would rectify the terrible indignity that had been done by the Wall.

As we stood there admiring it, Jim pointed out the dog tag laced into the boot of one of the statue's soldiers. "We used to do that so if your leg got blown off by a mine, they'd know whose it was." This was an arresting statement to someone who had spent the war conjugating irregular Latin verbs at a boarding school while Webb and his marines were taking—and giving back—withering fire in rice paddies. Jim told me of one comrade whose leg was blown off at the knee. The man stanched the bleeding by thrusting his stump into the mud and kept firing. Webb is a stern man with little tolerance for those who call, say, schoolteachers or single mothers "heroes."

Now the battle lines had been redrawn once again between Webb and Scruggs. Scruggs felt that this statue—which he had to pay for—was being foisted upon him. Moreover, he accused Hart, who had copyrighted and planned to sell replicas, of being in it mainly for the money. No one was speaking to each other. You hear the sound of incoming mortar rounds. The Left accused the Right of glorifying the war. The Right accused the Left of having dishonored the veterans in the first place.

Finally Rick Hart's statue passed the various committee hurdles. If you think getting a zoning variance for your swimming pool is hard, try getting something put on the Mall. The night before it was to be dedicated, on Veterans Day 1984, Jim Webb and Hart and the leading veterans who had fought fiercely against the Black V of Shame gathered at the Cosmos Club on Massachusetts Avenue to celebrate their victory. Tom Wolfe was there. Webb presented Hart, a nonveteran, with a marine sword, an impressive honor coming from Jim Webb. I have a memory of Rick holding it over his head, tears in his eyes, telling everyone that they had "fought the good fight, and prevailed!" Rick Hart died, way too soon, in 1999 at age 55. If you get to the National Cathedral, the arresting frieze called *Creation* above the main door, inspired by his reading of Jesuit philosopher Teilhard de Chardin, is his work. He left his mark on the city for all time.

The next day, in front of a large crowd of veterans, Jan Scruggs formally presented the statue to the United States government. In his remarks, he said, "It seems ironic. . . .

Instead of the Vietnam vets building a memorial and giving it to the government, the government should have built a memorial and given it to the vets. But then Vietnam was that kind of war." In the end, Jan fought not one, but two good fights.

LINCOLN MEMORIAL

I feel about the Lincoln Memorial the way T. S. Eliot felt about Shakespeare, namely that it's hopeless to try to say anything original about it; the best you can hope for is to be wrong about it in a new way. I doubt I'll even succeed at that.

If the Jefferson Memorial, with its graceful rotundity, is a one-man pantheon to a self-contented philosopher-intellectual, the Lincoln, with its hard angles, towering colonnade, and somber statue, is a temple to a martyr. The inscription above Daniel Chester French's statue proclaims:

IN THIS TEMPLE
AS IN THE HEARTS OF THE PEOPLE
FOR WHOM HE SAVED THE UNION
THE MEMORY OF ABRAHAM LINCOLN
IS ENSHRINED FOREVER

It was built over a filled-in swamp, in an area so desolate and forlorn that it seemed an insult to put it here. The Speaker of the House, "Uncle Joe" Cannon, harrumphed, "I'll never let a memorial to Abraham Lincoln be erected in that God-damned swamp." There is something reassuring about thwarted congressional asseverations.

What's perhaps more remarkable is that this site was once virtually the front line of the war that Mr. Lincoln fought and won. The South began on the other side of the river. What's more, just up the hill is Arlington House, the home of Robert E. Lee. For four years, the Union ended right here in the goop at the river's edge.

On reflection, maybe it's just as well that it takes forever to put up memorials in Washington. Rush jobs don't always turn out for the best. They certainly didn't rush this one. It wasn't completed until 1922.

Earlier plans called for another obelisk and a pyramid. One obelisk per capital seems about right, and no pyramid, however grand, is going to outdo Cheops's.

It was dedicated by President Harding. Chief Justice and former President William Howard Taft was there, as was President Lincoln's son, Robert Todd Lincoln, by then a distinguished-looking old man in neat white whiskers, spectacles, and, you can see from the photo, his father's large, signature ears. He was born in 1843, the year Samuel F. B. Morse stretched his first telegraph wire and Charles Dickens wrote *A Christmas Carol*. Now near the end of his life, there was little of American history that Robert Todd Lincoln had not personally witnessed.

After graduating from Harvard in 1864, he begged his father to let him enter the army so that he could take part in the war. The president had by this point lost two of his sons—another would die after he did, before reaching adulthood. He wasn't about to lose this one. Grant made him a member of his staff. Robert Lincoln was present at Appomattox on April 9, when Lee surrendered. Indeed, Lincoln's first eyewitness account of the occasion came from his son. Five days later, Robert was at his father's side when he died, nine hours after Booth fired the bullet into his brain.

That much I knew. What I did not know, until I read Philip Bigler's excellent book about Arlington National Cemetery, *In Honored Glory,* was this: In 1881, President Garfield appointed Robert Lincoln his secretary of war. Lincoln was with him at the Baltimore and Potomac Railroad Station when Garfield was shot. Twenty years later, in 1901, Robert Lincoln was present in Buffalo, New York, at the Pan-American Exposition when President McKinley was assassinated. This grim trifecta stands in apposition to his achievements: he became minister to Great Britain and a successful businessman. Alas, tragedy continued to haunt the Lincoln line. Robert's son Abraham "Jack" Lincoln II died at the age of 16. (The Lincoln line died out finally in 1985 with the death of Robert Todd Lincoln Beckwith.) Robert Todd Lincoln, the president's son, died in 1926, four years after witnessing one last momentous event, the dedication of his father's memorial. He is buried across the river, and we will pay our respects in due course.

Also present at the dedication that day was Dr. Robert Moton, president of the Tuskegee Institute. He was not allowed to sit on the speaker's platform. He had to go sit in the colored section. It's good to reflect that the wretched karma of this insult to the memory of Abraham Lincoln was finally exorcised 41 years later when Dr. Martin Luther King Jr. stood here in front of 200,000 people and said, "I have a dream."

Inside the Memorial, graven on the walls, are the only two speeches in American history that surpass Dr. King's: the Gettysburg Address and the Second Inaugural. I read the latter aloud to myself while standing there, quietly so as not to alarm anyone. It clocks in at under five minutes, bringing the total of those two orations to about seven minutes. Edward Everett, who also spoke at Gettysburg on November 19, 1863, wrote Lincoln afterward to say, "I should flatter myself if I thought that I came as close to the essence of the occasion in two hours as you did in two minutes."

What's notable about the Second Inaugural, apart from its eloquence ("With malice toward none, with charity for all"), is that it makes no specific mention of either North or South. Nor does it ascribe blame for the war, or even, for that matter, slavery. As Lincoln scholar David Herbert Donald notes, ". . . Lincoln had consistently held Northerners as well as Southerners responsible for introducing slavery and for protecting it under the Constitution."

Politicians who feel underappreciated can take comfort from the fact that although Lincoln was thunderously applauded when he sat down, most American newspapers gave it, according to Professor Donald, a "respectful, if somewhat puzzled reception." Lincoln was not too put out by the lukewarm reception. He observed that "men are not flattered by being shown that there has been a difference of purpose between the Almighty and them." William Dean Howells may have called Mark Twain "the Lincoln of our literature," but it's correspondingly true that Lincoln was the Twain of our politics. At any rate, Lincoln was delighted when he encountered Frederick Douglass at the reception afterward at the White House, where Douglass told him that his speech was "a sacred effort." When he tucked away his speech, Lincoln remarked to a friend, "Lots of wisdom in that document, I suspect."

Daniel Chester French, who sculpted the statue that stares out on the Reflecting Pool—just wait till old Abe gets a gander at that new World War II Memorial—set out to portray Lincoln as the Man of Burdens, reeling but erect, as G. K. Chesterton put it in another context. This is Lincoln as the Last Casualty of the War. French studied the life mask of Lincoln that you can see in the basement of the Memorial and it is hard to look upon the serenity of that noble plaster without being moved. When he left Springfield, Illinois, to come here, he said, "I now leave, not knowing when, or whether ever, I may return, with a task before me greater than that which rested upon Washington." When I first read that speech years ago as a schoolboy, I remember thinking how immodest that line sounded. Harder than what Washington faced? Come on!

Then years later I found myself here for the first time and saw the look on his face that French had captured, and understood.

Footnote: French knew and admired Edward Miner Gallaudet, son of Thomas Hopkins Gallaudet, founder of the first free public school for the deaf and later president of the college it became. Lincoln signed the bill that chartered Gallaudet College. French had a deaf son. Look at the hands on the statue. His left hand spells out in sign language the letter "A," his right the letter "L."

Walk Three

LAFAYETTE SQUARE

On the 137th anniversary of the day Mr. Lincoln was shot, I joined a tour in Lafayette Square conducted by an Englishman who loves the city as much as one of his countrymen once abominated it. Anthony Pitch, a spry man in floppy hat and mini vox loudspeaker, wrote a fine book about the British burning of Washington on August 24, 1814. He once saw, in the basement of the White House, the scorch marks left over from that episode. But for a thunderstorm that must have seemed heaven-sent, the entire city might have burned to the ground that day and become the Carthage of the new country. In fact—and this I learned from Jeanne Fogle's book *Proximity to Power* about this neighborhood—the White House became known as "The White House" three years after the burning, when it was painted white to cover up the torched exterior. Until then, it had had a distinctly pinkish hue owing to the iron in the Aquia Creek sandstone used to build it. (Remember where we stood on Aquia Creek sandstone? That's right, in the Capitol Rotunda.) But the president's house didn't become officially known as "The White House" until Teddy Roosevelt decided that that's what he wanted on the stationery. So just as we might have called it "Hamburger Hill," if Thomas Jefferson had had his way, the British in the end spared us from calling it "The Pink House." We're in debt, then, to Rear Admiral Cockburn for his otherwise disgraceful behavior. His descendant, Andrew Cockburn, lives here, in Georgetown, and so far hasn't set fire to anything other than right wingers.

But today, Tony Pitch's theme is Abraham Lincoln, and his enthusiasm for the man is little short of idolatrous. "He was one of the most amazing people who ever walked the earth," says Mr. Pitch, intense blue eyes all alive. "He was self-taught and never took umbrage at insults. That such a man was shot, in the back the head, is one of the most *monstrous insults that ever happened.*" I liked Mr. Pitch right away.

We walked over to the White House and peered through the fence at the North Portico. He pointed out the center window on the second floor. (You can see it on a $20 bill.) On April 11, 1865, he told us, Abraham Lincoln appeared through that window and gave a speech. "It was the first time he had said aloud that blacks should get the vote." A 26-year-old actor named John Wilkes Booth was in the crowd outside, along with a man named Lewis Paine. Booth had been stalking Lincoln for weeks.

Booth growled, "That means nigger citizenship. That is the last speech he will ever make. . . . By God, I'll put him through."

Another man was in the crowd that day, a 23-year-old doctor named Leale.

Tony pointed out another window, two over (that is, to the right). "That room was called the Prince of Wales Room. That's where they did the autopsy and the embalming."

My mind went back 20 years, to a night I had dinner in that room, seated at a small table with President Reagan and two authentic royal princesses, both of them daughters of American actresses (Rita Hayworth and Grace Kelly). I mention this not to make you think, Well whupty-do for *you*, Mr. Snooty. Let me emphasize: 99.98 percent of my dinners in those days took place at a Hamburger Hamlet or McDonald's or over my kitchen sink. But at one point in this heady meal, President Reagan turned to one of the princesses and remarked that his Cavalier King Charles spaniel, Rex, would begin barking furiously whenever he came into this room. There was no explaining it, he said. Then he told about Lincoln and suddenly the President of the United States and the two princesses began swapping ghost stories and I was left with a voice in my ear whispering, *I don't think we're in Kansas anymore, Toto.*

After the dinner, the pianist Michael Feinstein played in the solarium overlooking the Monument and the Jefferson in the distance. Before Feinstein played, the president introduced him graciously, mentioning that it was right here on this spot that the leg of President Truman's piano went through the floor, prompting an urgent architectural review that resulted in a 27-month-long gutting and renovation of the White House. That's why you'll find a plaque outside Blair House across the street on Pennsylvania Avenue in honor of Secret Service agent Leslie Coffelt, who on November 1, 1950, engaged in and was mortally wounded during a two-minute gun battle with Puerto Rican extremists who had come to kill President Truman. He and the First Family were living at Blair House during the renovation. Everything's connected in Washington, one way or another.

As our theme is Lincoln, it's worth noting that it was at Blair House that Robert E. Lee turned down the command of the Union Army, on the grounds that he could never raise arms against his beloved Virginia.

For two years, I had a White House pass that allowed me everywhere except, of course, the second floor residence. One time, hearing that Jimmy Cagney was about to get the Medal of Freedom in the East Room—where Abigail Adams hung out her wash to dry, where Lincoln's body lay in state, and where I once sat behind *Dynasty* star Joan Collins while she and husband number four (I think it was) spelunked in each other's mouths with their tongues, while Andy Williams crooned "Moon River"— I rushed over from the Old Executive Office Building just in time to see President Reagan pin it on the man who had tapped out "Yankee Doodle Dandy" and was now a sad, crumpled, speechless figure in a wheelchair. I remember Reagan putting his hand on Cagney's shoulder and saying how generous he had been "many years ago to a young contract player on the Warner Brothers lot."

I was back in that same room a decade later to watch his successor award my father with the same medal. Another recipient that day was Ted Williams, who died just a few days ago as I write this. I have his autograph on the White House menu, and only if all else fails will I hawk it on eBay. He wasn't in the least happy about being asked for it.

Another time during the administration of George H.W. Bush, I was in the audience in the State Dining Room for a talk about Lincoln's time at the White House by Professor David Herbert Donald.

I was sitting directly behind Colin Powell, then Chairman of the Joint Chiefs of Staff, and remember that for one hour General Powell did not move *one centimeter.* That's military bearing. What I also remember of the evening was Professor Donald's stories about Mary Todd Lincoln's extravagances. Mrs. Lincoln was the Imelda Marcos of her day. This woman *shopped.* Among her purchases was the enormous rosewood bed that became known as the Lincoln Bed, even though her husband never spent a night in it. The Lincoln Bedroom became notorious during the Clinton years as a sort of Motel 6 for big party donors. At any rate, by 1864, Mary Todd Lincoln had run up a monumental bill. While field commanders were shouting "Charge!" Mrs. Lincoln had been saying, "Charge it!" She faced disaster the moment her husband stopped being president, this being when shop-keepers tended to hold out their hands for payment.

Lincoln vacillated over whether to run for a second term. The war still raged on, his popularity was low. Many thought he shouldn't. Not Mary Lincoln! She was 100 percent for a second term. *But Abe, dear, the country* needs *you!*

Professor Donald ended his riveting talk by looking rather wistfully toward the front door. He said that Mrs. Lincoln hadn't wanted to go to the theater that night. But the newspapers had advertised that Lincoln would attend, and the president felt obliged to those who had come expecting to see him. In his excellent book *April 1865,* historian Jay Winik writes that Abe wanted to relax and "have a laugh over *The Country Cousin.*" Never has a decision to go to the theater been so consequential.

"And so," said Professor Donald, "they left the White House together for the last time."

Let's rejoin Tony Pitch's tour now.

We're standing in Lafayette Square in front of a red brick building, Number 712 Jackson Place. The plaque notes that it's the Commission on White House Fellow-ships, the one-year government internship program for promising young aspirants. Colin Powell was one. In April 1865 it was the residence of a young army major named Henry Rathbone, who was engaged to his stepsister Clara, daughter of a New York senator.

As Professor Donald recounts in his Lincoln biogra-phy, April 14, 1865, was a Good Friday, not a big night to go out, traditionally. It's hard to imagine today, when an invitation from the President of the United States is tantamount to a subpoena, but the Lincolns had a hard time finding people to go out with them that night. His own secretary of war, Edwin Stanton, declined. (Mrs. Stanton couldn't stand Mrs. Lincoln.) General Grant also begged off. (Mrs. Grant also couldn't stand Mrs. Lincoln.) Lincoln was subsequently turned down by a governor, another general, the Detroit postmaster (!), another governor (Idaho Territory), and the chief of the telegraph bureau at the War Department, an army major named Eckert. At this point, poor Abe was so desperate that he was reduced to cajoling. The image of him pleading with an army major to come sit in the president's box is the final (tragi-)comic vignette we have of Lincoln. It's of a piece with his humanity and humility. But by gum, Eckert held his ground—there was too much work to do. So finally Abe turned to another army major, Henry Rathbone. Rathbone said to the president, Okay, okay, whatever.

After John Wilkes Booth shot Lincoln, Rathbone lunged for him. Booth sank a viciously sharp 7¼-inch blade into his arm, opening a wound from elbow to shoulder. Rathbone managed to survive, but the wound went deeper. Eighteen years later, as U.S. consul general in Hanover, Germany, he went into the room of his wife, Clara, one night and shot her dead. Rathbone died 28 years later in an asylum for the criminally insane. "He was one of the many people," Tony said, "whose lives were broken that night."

As we walked away, one of the other people on the tour, a heavily bejeweled woman with bright red hair, dark glasses, skin-tight black pants, and high heels that seemed unusual for a two-hour walking tour on a warm day, turned to her companion, "Did he say he went crazy and shot his wife? If he was crazy, why didn't he shoot himself? What's *that* all about?"

Tony pointed out the Old Executive Office Building next to the White House. The building that stood here in Lincoln's time was the War Department. Lincoln spent a lot of his time here with Major Eckert, sending and receiving telegraphs to and from his generals in the field.

EISENHOWER EXECUTIVE OFFICE BUILDING

The second Bush administration renamed the OEOB the Eisenhower Executive Office Building, which to my mind is a bit much, since in 1957 Ike's administration wanted to tear the building down and put up a ghastly modern replacement. The Kennedy crew put a stop to that, thank heavens, as well as to plans to tear down an entire row of historic houses on Lafayette Square. Twenty years later, Mrs. Kennedy would play a significant role in stopping the tearing down of another American Beauty, New York City's Grand Central Terminal.

The OEOB—which I still insist on calling it—is my favorite building in Washington. It's a gaudy old pile, to be sure. Technically, it's French Second Empire, but it's been called other things: Victorian wedding cake, "the greatest monstrosity in America" (by Harry Truman), "Mr. Mullett's architectural infant asylum" (Henry Adams). Me, I calls it grand.

It looks a bit like the Denon Pavilion of the Louvre in Paris, only more so. When it was finished in 1888, at the height of the Gilded Age, it was the Pentagon of its day, the world's largest office building, with two miles of corridors, 556 rooms, and 900 columns. According to Applewhite, those 26 concrete Grecian urn–type flowerpots you see were added by Army Captain Douglas MacArthur when he was superintendent of the building in 1913. You don't usually think of "MacArthur" and "flowerpots" in the same sentence, do you?

This is where my office was, in a room with a majestic view of—an interior courtyard parking lot. Into the bargain, it was being resurfaced. Being a U.S. government project, this took 18 months, so my enduring memory of my days of power and glory is the sound of jackhammers and a window-unit air conditioner that rattled and dripped onto the shag rug next to my electric typewriter.

I'm sure there's a plaque up on Room 205 to commemorate my historic tenure, but the OEOB is possibly better known for having provided office space for 25 secretaries of state, including John Hay, William Jennings Bryan, Cordell Hull, and George C. Marshall; and for 21 secretaries of war, including Robert Todd Lincoln and Henry Stimson.

Since Lyndon Johnson's time, vice presidents of the United States have had an office on the second floor overlooking the West Wing of the White House. Vice President Walter Mondale nicknamed the OEOB "Baltimore" because it was so remote from the real power, that is, about a hundred feet away in the West Wing. The VP's office was renovated while I worked here, and after painstaking work was restored to the glory it enjoyed when it had been the office of Assistant Secretary of the Navy Theodore Roosevelt and later, General John J. "Blackjack" Pershing. A poor Secret Service agent had to sit there *every day* for nearly a year while the workmen labored, to make sure they didn't plant any bugs.

Even after two years of going into that office, I never lost my awe of the place. Mr. Bush's desk had been used by all the vice presidents, and before they left office it was the custom for them to write their names in the drawer. Mr. Bush would show it to visitors. In staff meetings, Mr. Bush would sit in an armchair and didn't mind if one of us sat in his desk chair. I never dared, but one time someone who did accidentally touched an alarm button with his knees and the Secret Service came rushing in through three doors.

There's history in every square foot of the Old Exec. It was originally called the State, War and Navy Building. You could tell from the emblem on the doorknobs— eagle, crest, anchor—what wing you were in. You'd be in some boring meeting with the deputy assistant for whatever and someone would say, "Wasn't this Hull's office?" and it would turn out that sure enough, it was right here that he summoned the Japanese envoys Nomura and

Korusu on December 7, 1941, and tore them new orifices. Or you'd be in another boring meeting and that office would turn out to have been Nixon's hideaway, where he went to get away and to scribble his endless, endless memos to Haldeman and Ehrlichman on yellow legal pads.

The two miles of corridors are tiled in black and white and if you look down as you walk, you'll see little fossils embedded in them. My girlfriend at the time also worked in the building and I still remember the sound of her high heels approaching my office door.

It was in the basement of the OEOB that new staffers who traveled with their principal got a briefing by the Secret Service on how to stay alive. This was just after Hinckley shot President Reagan and crippled Jim Brady for life, so we did pay attention. Basically, the briefing consisted of home assassination movies, with expert narration. We saw the Zapruder film of the Kennedy assassination, backward and forward, in slow motion; saw Arthur Bremer unloading his pistol into George Wallace, paralyzing him for life. The one I remember most vividly was of an attempt on President Park Chung Hee of South Korea. He's giving a speech, surrounded by security men. Someone runs down the aisle, pulls out a pistol, and begins blazing away. President Park coolly ducks behind the podium, while a fierce gun battle ensues. Then one of his security guards takes cover onstage—behind Mrs. Park. And surprise, she's killed. I thought it was an interesting career move on the security man's part. The Secret

Service agent narrating this tragic Keystone Kop drama observed, "*We* don't do it this way."

When the lights went up, the basement room was very quiet. The agent said, "If something happens, you basically have two choices: duck, or take the round." I said, "*What* was the first choice again?" Fond as I already was of Mr. Bush, I was pretty sure that if it came to that, I would opt for Option One.

The OEOB was the creation of an English immigrant architect named Alfred B. Mullett. Poor old Mullett worked 17 years building his masterpiece only to end up suing the government. He felt overworked and underpaid. The government said, Get lost, and Mullet shot himself. His ghost is supposed to wander the two miles of corridors, but I never saw it, even though I spent many late nights in the place.

Let's rejoin Tony by the statue of Andrew Jackson. You can't miss it: it's smack in the middle of . . .

LAFAYETTE PARK

It started out as "President's Park." Before that it was an apple orchard. This was originally the White House's front lawn, until Thomas Jefferson decided it was all too much and bisected the property with a road he called Executive Way. You know it as Pennsylvania Avenue.

It was here, according to Jeanne Fogle's *Proximity to Power,* that the first Fourth of July celebration was held, in 1801. Jefferson was determined to make it a *loud*

celebration of our independence. It featured events to
offend every modern sensibility: gunfire, cockfights, dog-
fights. It was all such fun that the new nation couldn't wait
for the next Fourth of July. The Republican Ladies of Che-
shire, Massachusetts, sent a 1,200-pound cheese to the president. America being America, we took this idea and ran
with it. A second enormous cheese was sent to celebrate
Washington's birthday. By 1837, the cheese had grown to
1,400 pounds. It was placed in a White House vestibule,
where the citizenry shaved and hacked and scooped away
at it, leaving arguably the worst mess in American history.
Only a meager sliver remained for the commander in chief.
Today if you sent the president a cheese of this size the
Secret Service would arrest you for attempted assassination by cholesterol. When President George H. W. Bush
declared that he hated broccoli and, gosh darnit, wasn't
going to eat it anymore now that he was the most powerful
man in the world, the nation's broccoli growers dumped
several forklifts full on the White House lawn. We progress.

President's Park became known as Lafayette Park (or
Square) after a triumphant return visit to America by the
Marquis de Lafayette. Marie-Joseph-Paul-Yves-Roch-
Gilbert du Motier, Marquis de Lafayette—Gilbert to his
friends—had been a wealthy, if orphaned, 19-year-old
officer in the French army. He read the Declaration of
Independence and decided it was a far, far greater thing
than making Europe safe for a feckless overweight Bour-
bon king. Louis XVI, *naturellement,* had other views, and
forbade the impetuous young man from leaving his

service. But Gilbert was determined and joined up. He proved himself and was soon major general and Washington's aide-de-camp at Valley Forge, where he surely was acquainted with his countryman L'Enfant, the Continental Army's "artist extraordinary." Lafayette not only fought for us, but got aid and volunteers from France, and it was he who forced British General Cornwallis to beat a retreat to Yorktown and surrender. He returned to France after our Revolution, only to get caught up in another. He designed the French tricolor flag. He ended up a prisoner of war in Austria for five years, but made it through and became commander of the National Guard. There's a scene in the movie *Patton* where George C. Scott, as Patton, gives a speech in fluent French, telling the crowd that he is impatient to liberate France, *"Le pays natal de Lafayette!"*

Gilbert's return to Washington made Charles Lindbergh's ticker-tape parade down Broadway look like a midnight sneak through the service entrance. The procession was two miles long. Flowers were literally strewn in his path. The $200,000 that he had spent out of his own pocket helping us was returned to him, along with a generous grant of land. This victory lap went on for a year, and included a visit to Washington's tomb at Mount Vernon, an occasion treated with the greatest solemnity.

This visit took place in 1824. One wonders what poor old L'Enfant, eating corncobs out in Bladensburg to the sound of duelists blasting away at each other, made of this elaborate *vernissage*. He died in 1825. Lafayette's triumph must have finished him off.

Lafayette got the front lawn of the White House named after him. L'Enfant Plaza, meanwhile, is over in Southwest D.C., hidden behind the Energy Department and U.S. Postal Service, which is just as well, since it looks as though it was designed by Stalin. A grateful nation honors the man who designed its capital.

I hadn't known about the Curse of Lafayette Square until I took Tony Pitch's tour that day. It turns out to be Washington's Bermuda Triangle. A significant number of people who lived here ended up shot, stabbed, or dead by their own hand. Major Rathbone you know about, and Clover Adams, wife of Henry, who lived where the Hay-Adams Hotel is now and who swallowed a bottle of potassium cyanide in 1885, distraught over the death of her father. Her husband never spoke of it; after he died in 1918, they found the bottle in his desk drawer. He had kept it as a tragic *memento mori*.

On the northwest corner of the park is Decatur House, a dignified square red brick Federal. Decatur was the naval hero of his day, having distinguished himself in the war against the Barbary pirates of Tripoli—("From the Halls of Mon-te-zu-oo-ma, to the shores of Tri-po-li . . ."). In those days, you got a bonus for capturing enemy ships, so he returned from his wars a wealthy man. The government might consider reinstituting this practice.

When Decatur hired Benjamin Latrobe, around 1817, to build him a residence, this area was far from being a posh neighborhood. It wasn't really even a neighborhood. But Decatur liked the idea of living just up the street from the President of the United States. He and his beautiful wife, Susan, became the A-list couple of their day.

It didn't last long. In 1820, a former American naval commodore named James Barron, still smarting over Decatur's vote against him in a court-martial for incompetence, challenged him to a duel. What an awful pain in the butt duels must have been. But the dictates of honor left you little choice but to accept.

They met at dawn on the dueling grounds just over the District line in Bladensburg, and shot each other. Barron took one in the hip. Decatur got his in the chest.

They brought him back to the smart house on President's Park and there he soon died. His wife, Susan, was so distraught she couldn't bear to be with him. He was a stallion to the end. His dying words were, "If it were in the cause of my country, it would be nothing." Susan became a recluse and according to one account, "grew old wringing her hands and weeping for her lost husband." So there's a story to cheer you up on a rainy day. Sorry.

Next to the Decatur House on the street now named Jackson Place once stood the home of a New York congressman named Daniel Sickles. He married a much younger, pretty woman named Teresa, daughter of an Italian music teacher—and you can tell right away where this is going.

Being the much younger wife of a politician who would rather talk about tariffs with other politicians instead of, say, drinking Champagne, reading the sonnets of Shakespeare by candlelight, and making mad, passionate love, Teresa grew a bit restless. She met the Honorable Philip Barton Key at a dinner party at the Sickleses' then-new residence. Key was the district attorney for the District of Columbia, and the son of Francis Scott Key, the Maryland lawyer who on the morning of September 14, 1814, three weeks after the burning of Washington, looked out the porthole of the ship he was being detained on and saw the star-spangled banner still waving over Fort McHenry.

Teresa and Philip were soon reading sonnets in a rented house just off Lafayette Square, and doing the other thing. They worked out a signal: they would wave white han-kies at each other, Teresa from her window, Philip from the other end of Lafayette Square, or as he walked by the house.

All good things come to an end. Someone tipped off Congressman Sickles. One February morning in 1859, he saw the Honorable Key waving his hanky in the direction of his wife's window, and went ballistic. Very literally. He charged out, shouting, "Key, you scoundrel, you have dis-honored my house—you must die!" Today this sounds like dialogue from a badly dubbed kung fu movie, but back then it must have sounded impressive. Sickles fired one round into the Honorable Key, who fled, as best he could. Sickles followed and shot him again. The Honor-able Key was now cowering at the base of a tree. What else could he do, other than to hurl his opera glasses at Sickles. A feckless gesture, but one uses the tools at hand. Sickles, undeterred by the flying opera glasses, fired a third time. The Honorable Key was carried into the Washington Club, where he presently died.

Sickles was put on trial. Being a man of substance, he hired himself the best legal talent there was—Edwin Stanton, whom we'll meet again at the end of this walk. Stanton defended Sickles on the grounds that he was not himself by reason of a "temporary aberration of mind," the first instance in America of what would become known as the insanity defense. It was used not long ago to acquit a defendant in another Washington shooting that took place not far from here. John Hinckley remains at St. Elizabeths Hospital, the most notorious inmate there since the poet Ezra Pound, who spent 13 years there after being acquitted of treason for his World War II pro-fascist radio broadcasts.

Sickles was acquitted, took Teresa back, though the magic had definitely gone out of this marriage. He went on to fight at the Battle of Gettysburg, where he lost his left leg. He had it preserved and for years on the anniversary of the amputation would go, often with friends, to visit it at the Army Medical Museum, where the Hirshhorn Donut now stands. Later, President Grant made him United States Minister to Spain. No one would have said to Daniel Sickles, "Get a life."

Several years later, the house in which the Honorable Key bled to death all over the upholstery became the home of William H. Seward, President Lincoln's secretary of state. On the night of April 14, 1865, he was at home recovering from terrible injuries sustained in a carriage accident. Lewis Paine rang the bell, claiming to have brought medication from the apothecary. Seward's son Frederick sensed that something was not right here and challenged him. Paine's revolver jammed. He pistol-whipped the younger Seward and then made his way upstairs and began carving up the old man with a Bowie knife. Servants intervened, getting themselves stabbed and knocked senseless. The carnage was appalling. It was a miracle that either Seward survived. The son wore a cap for the rest of his life to conceal his scars. Bear this in mind when we come to a certain exhibit in the basement of Ford's Theater.

If you're not too depressed by now, let's make quick stops at two more sites, much more cheerful. See, they're even both painted a cheery yellow.

First is the house at the northeast corner of the park. This was the home of former President James Madison and his wife, Dolley. The only object that has been in the White House continuously—with one notable interruption— since the mansion was occupied in 1800 is the "Lansdowne" full-length portrait of George Washington by Gilbert Stuart. It hangs in the East Room.

We owe that to Mrs. Madison, who refused to leave the White House without the painting, even as the torch-bearing Brits approached. She wrote to her sister that day: "Our kind friend, Mr. Carroll, has come to hasten my departure, and is in a very bad humor with me because I insist on waiting until the large picture of Gen. Washington is secured, and it requires to be unscrewed from the wall. This process was found too tedious for these perilous moments; I have ordered the frame to be broken, and the canvas taken out; it is done . . . And now, dear sister, I must leave this house, or the retreating army will make me a prisoner in it. . . ."

I was hoping to leave it at that, but then Tony Pitch pointed out that her son by her first husband "was a scoundrel. He took paintings out of her house as she was dying." The curse, again. A sad fate for the Lady who performed such a heroic office for her country.

One block west, on the corner of 16th and H Streets, is St. John's Church. Every time you see the U.S. president on television going in or coming out of a church, chances are it's this one. Dolley Madison encouraged the idea of a church here, and it was completed in 1816. She was baptized here into the Episcopalian faith and eulogized here during her funeral services. Every president since her husband has worshiped here. Whether this record will continue in the event of a Joe Lieberman presidency, we'll just have to see. It's a cozy, creaky space, designed by the handsome, busy Benjamin Latrobe, who left his mark on so much in Washington: the Capitol Building, White House, Navy Yard, Decatur House, as well as many other residences. In a letter to his son, he wrote, "I have just completed a church that made many Washingtonians religious who had not been religious before." The bell in the steeple was melted down from a British cannon and is rung when a president dies in office.

Let's conclude our Lafayette walk here, lest we trip over some other depressing doorstep and Tony starts telling us about a horrible massacre that took place on it.

But we began with Lincoln and should, properly, end with him, so if you would, walk east on H Street for seven blocks, then turn right on 10th and go two-and-a-half blocks, into Ford's Theater.

FORD'S THEATER

I had last been here on my second date with the beautiful CIA officer who eventually agreed to marry me. The play was a comedy, but even as I chuckled, I kept looking up at the box. I don't know how any actor can manage to get through a play here. Talk about negative energy. And it didn't stop with the dreadful night of April 14, 1865. Ford's later became a government office building and one day in 1893 a floor collapsed, killing 22 people.

They used to let you walk up the narrow passageway to the box and see with your own eyes what Booth saw. It's an impressive leap he made from the box after shooting Lincoln—11-plus feet, but as a trained actor, he might have landed without injury if only he hadn't caught a heel on the flag draped over the president's box. Professor Donald quotes a witness who described Booth's motion across the stage as "like the hopping of a bullfrog." That broken leg led to the imprisonment of the man who set it, Dr. Samuel Mudd. My next-door neighbor, an attractive, genial fellow surnamed Mudd, is a relative of the doctor.

The artifacts are in the basement museum. The .44-caliber single-shot pistol made by Derringer of Philadelphia, the knife Booth plunged into Rathbone's artery, the Brooks Brothers coat made for Lincoln's second inaugural, the left sleeve torn away by relic-hunters, the size 14 boots, the bloodstained towels.

Booth was tracked down and shot to death on April 26. The conspirators were hanged on July 9. My wife's great-great-grandfather was one of the guards you see in the photograph by the gallows. And over here are the manacles and handcuffs the conspirators wore in prison while awaiting their execution. Here, too, are the white canvas hoods they wore to prevent them from communicating with each other. In Washington, inevitably, one thinks of the heat. There's a letter beneath one of the hoods. It's from Brevet Major General John F. Hartranft, commandant of the military prison, dated June 6, 1865: "The prisoners are suffering very much from the padded hoods and I would respectfully request that they be removed from all the prisoners, except 195." This was Lewis Paine, Seward's attacker. There's a photograph of him (not here) showing Paine in manacles, staring coldly and remorselessly at the photographer. Perhaps it was this stare that persuaded Maj. Gen. Hartranft that the hood was best left on.

I crossed the street to the House Where Lincoln Died. I had been here as a child and remembered with a child's ghoulish but innocent fascination the blood-drenched pillow. It was gone now. I asked the National Park Service ranger what had happened to it. "It's been removed to a secure location," she said. "Secure location"? I thought of the final scene in the movie *Raiders of the Lost Ark,* as the

Ark is being wheeled away to be stored amid a zillion other boxes in a vast government warehouse. She added, "It was deteriorating." Okay, but for heaven's sake don't tell me where it is, or I might steal it.

The air is close and musty inside. The little sign on the table says simply, "President Lincoln died in this room at 7:22 A.M. on April 15, 1865." You automatically reach to remove your hat. Lincoln was six-foot-four. They had to lie him down on the bed diagonally, with his knees slightly bent. He lived for nine hours.

I went back outside. Tony was telling the story. Charles Leale, the 23-year-old army surgeon who had been in the crowd outside the White House when Lincoln made the speech that inflamed Booth, was the first doctor to reach the box. He located the wound and knew right away it was mortal. He removed the clot that had formed, to relieve pressure on the president's brain. Leale said that the rough ride over cobblestones back to the White House would surely kill him, so they carried him across the street. According to historian Shelby Foote, Mrs. Lincoln was asked to leave the room after she shrieked when she saw Lincoln's face twitch and the bullet-affected eye bulging out from its socket.

Secretary of War Stanton—Dan Sickles's former lawyer—arrived and set up in the adjoining parlor and took statements. They could not keep up with the note-taking, so the crowd outside was asked if anyone knew shorthand. A man named James Tanner stepped forward and volunteered. Tanner had lost both legs at the Second

Battle of Manassas in 1862 but, wanting to go on contributing to the war effort, had taken up stenography. We'll pay our respects to him when we get to Arlington. He took notes through the night. He recalled later, "In fifteen minutes I had enough down to hang John Wilkes Booth."

Jackie Kennedy, Mrs. Lincoln was not. She kept wailing and crying, "Why didn't they kill me?" and "Is he dead? Oh, is he dead?" The last straw was when she shrieked and fainted after the unconscious Lincoln released a loud exhalation when she was by his face. Stanton shouted, "Take that woman out and do not let her in again!"

Dr. Leale had seen many men die of head wounds. He knew that they sometimes regained consciousness just before dying. He also knew that if the president did regain consciousness, he would be blind. He held the president's hand so that he would at least feel the presence of another human being in his final moments. At 7:22 in the morning it was over and Stanton said, "Now he belongs to the ages." Dr. Leale walked back to his boardinghouse in the drizzle in his bloodstained clothes.

Mrs. Surratt's boardinghouse, where the conspirators hatched their plot, is not far, near the corner of H and 6th Streets. It's a Chinese restaurant called Wok & Roll.

Walk Four

ARLINGTON NATIONAL CEMETERY

Our last walk ended on a solemn note, and now that we're crossing Arlington Memorial Bridge on our way to Arlington National Cemetery you must be thinking that this is turning into Buckley's Death March. Bear with me. It may be a cemetery, but it's also a place to lift the spirits and refresh the old soul. Your money back if don't end up proud of your country and, at a minimum, thrilled still to be alive.

But before we get to Arlington, stop for a moment. (Do not do this if you are in a car halfway across the bridge. It will only annoy the other cars.) I just want to point out a couple things.

First, we're crossing the river right about where George Washington crossed it with Braddock back in 1755 on their way to fight the French.

Exciting, huh? Do you need a snack or something? All right, then maybe this will get your motor running. See that mansion up the hill ahead of you, the one that looks like it was modeled on the Temple of Poseidon at Paestum? What a relief—finally, a building *not* modeled on the Pantheon in Rome. Well, the first major military action of the Civil War wasn't Bull Run, but the movement of 14,000 Union troops on the night of May 23, 1861, across the river here to occupy that house and the land around it.

It belonged to Robert E. Lee. The property had belonged to his wife's family, she being the daughter of George Washington's step-grandson. His wife bore six of his seven children there. At any rate, the army wasn't occupying it just to make a personal point, but to prevent Confederate forces from using the high ground as an artillery platform from which to bombard the capital. The element of personal spite would enter in later.

In 1864, the Union began burying its dead along the driveway leading up to the house. By the end of the war, there were 16,000 dead buried around the house. The bones of 2,111 unidentified men from Bull Run were buried in Mary Lee's rose garden.

You have to go back to ancient Rome or Greece to find a more chilling act of revenge. Cato's cry, "Carthage must be destroyed!" was well known to Quartermaster General of the Army Montgomery C. Meigs. Meigs hated Robert E. Lee, and he had a personal reason for hating him: his son had been killed in the war. So this vast necropolis is a father's act of settling the score. You'll recall that one of Meigs's previous achievements was to help with the completion of the dome over the Capitol. These two very different undertakings of his provide the city with its antipodes. One rises to the sky, the other sinks into the earth.

"From the heavy brick porch they looked across the superb river to the raw and incoherent ugliness of the city," Henry Adams wrote in his anonymously published novel, *Democracy,* "idealized into dreamy beauty by the atmosphere, and the soft background of purple hills beyond. Opposite them, with its crude 'thus saith the law' stamped on white dome and fortress-like walls, rose the Capitol."

The novel is set in 1868, just three years after the war ended. Sybil and Carrington have driven out here for a picnic. Sybil is appalled at the condition of the Lee mansion. "How awfully sad it is!" she says. Carrington muses, ". . . I never thought we could be beaten. Yet now I am sitting here a pardoned rebel, and the poor Lees are driven away and their place is a graveyard."

I'm standing right where this fictional conversation took place, in front of the ocher Greek Revival manse. A tour guide is doing his best to hold the attention of several hundred high schoolers.

"Four weeks before he was killed," the guide says, struggling to be heard above Discmans pumping Eminem and P. Diddy, "President Kennedy and his wife were here for the funeral of a high-ranking military man. And afterward, they strolled RIGHT HERE and looked out and

President Kennedy said, 'WOULDN'T THIS BE A GREAT PLACE TO BE BURIED?' And Mrs. Kennedy remembered that. She got the idea for the eternal flame from Gettysburg. WHO HERE HAS BEEN TO GETTYSBURG?"

According to Philip Bigler's *In Honored Glory,* Secretary of Defense Robert McNamara came to Arlington the day after President Kennedy was murdered to scout sites. He was shown three possible sites: near the mast of the USS *Maine,* Dewey Circle, and the slope here below the Arlington House. Bobby Kennedy chose the latter site, and Mrs. Kennedy arrived later in the day and approved it. It was only then that a Park Service employee pointed out that the president had visited the mansion on March 3 of that year. He remarked to his friend Charlie Bartlett that it was so magnificent, he could stay here forever. So as it turned out, Bobby Kennedy and Mrs. Kennedy had chosen well.

A Lieutenant Samuel Bird was in charge of the "Old Guard" that would carry the heavy casket. They would have to negotiate the steep steps of the Capitol Building, where the president had lain in state, as well as those of St. Matthew's Cathedral, then Arlington. Lieutenant Bird was anxious that his men might drop it, so shortly after midnight, he convened his men on the steps of the Tomb of the Unknowns. A casket was filled with sandbags, and they practiced carrying it up and down the steps, over and over, with Lieutenant Bird and another soldier sitting on top for added weight. It went without a hitch the next day.

Actually, just one: the broadcast media kept filming as they began to lower the coffin into the ground after the ceremony. They were not supposed to do this. The furious superintendent solved the problem by shutting off their electricity. There were 23 other burials at Arlington on November 25, 1963. Death, as life, goes on.

Sixteen million people visited the grave over the next three years, causing chaos and the inevitable vandalism, and forcing a redesign. On March 14, 1967, a secret reinterment took place. The president and his two deceased children were moved 20 feet down the slope from the original grave beneath a new granite plaza planted with sedum and fescue. All this I learned from Mr. Bigler's book.

There was, as always, a crowd when I got there. Mrs. Kennedy is now there, and the crowds seemed to me denser than they were before 1994, when she was buried beside her husband and children. Across the river, at the Corcoran Museum, an exhibit about her was solidly sold out. A week before, on a bit of a lark, I'd signed on for a walking tour named "Jackie Kennedy's Georgetown." When I showed up, there were five times the number of people there had been on the Lincoln tour. I'll let you take that tour on your own but will just point out that the last house she lived in in Washington, before the curiosity seekers drove her to New York, is on N Street, right across from a house once occupied by Robert Todd Lincoln.

I paid my respects, then walked about 20 feet, to the north, to visit an old friend, Allard K. Lowenstein. Al had been a one-term congressman from New York, and a fierce opponent of the Vietnam War. He was a kind of Pied Piper, full of passion, and he motivated hordes of young people to get involved in politics. Once, at the Republican Convention in Kansas City in 1976, I heard a knock on my hotel room door at two in the morning. I opened it and it was Al, needing a couch to crash on. For some reason, he tossed his yarmulke at me and said I could keep it. I laughed at this strange payment for a night's rental of my couch. I still have it somewhere.

Four years later, he was dead. One of those youthful followers had become convinced that Al and the CIA and God knows who else were controlling him through his dental filings. He walked into Al's office in Rockefeller Center and pumped five bullets into his chest. The memorial service at the Central Synagogue on Lexington Avenue was standing-room only, the crowd spilling out onto the street, stopping traffic.

The first time I came to visit him here, I followed the directions they gave me, and found him here, right next to the Kennedys. Only Al could have managed that. He loved Bobby Kennedy. It made me smile. The words on his stone say:

ALLARD K. LOWENSTEIN
PFC US ARMY
JANUARY 16, 1929–MARCH 14, 1980

If a single man plant himself on his convictions and there abide, the huge world will come round to him.

I said good-bye to Al and walked up a pathway and some stairs leading back up to the mansion. On the way, I came across a very old grave within a red brick wall enclosure. A plaque advertises it as the grave of the first person ever buried at Arlington, Mary Randolph. It says that Mary was a "direct descendant of Pocahontas, cousin of Thomas Jefferson and of Mary Lee Fitzhugh Custis, wife of George Washington Parke Custis," who built the mansion just up the path. I read on: her youngest son had been a U.S. Navy midshipman and was crippled in a fall from a mast. "Her devoted care of that injured son is said to have hastened her death and would seem to explain her epitaph." In a pathetic imitation of Spider-Man, I crawled over the red brick wall and let myself down. I felt like a grave robber, but I wanted to read the inscription. Alas, the flat stone atop her grave had long since crumbled to illegibility. I rested my hand on the granular surface and then climbed out and made my way to the Tomb of the Unknowns.

I remember the day in May 1984 when they finally buried the Unknown from the Vietnam War. It had been difficult to find one in the age of sophisticated forensic analysis, but in due course they had located remains that they could not identify. They lay in state in the Capitol Building over the Memorial Day weekend. A quarter million people filed past. President Reagan spoke at Arlington. He concluded, "Let us, if we must, debate the lessons learned at some other time. Today we simply say with pride, Thank you, dear son, and may God cradle you in

His loving arms." In the silence that settled over the marble plaza, you could hear people choking back sobs.

Fourteen years later, in 1998, the remains they interred that day were identified by DNA analysis as belonging to Air Force Captain Michael Blassie, shot down May 11, 1972, over the jungle. He was disinterred and returned to his family for burial in St. Louis. The tomb remains empty, a symbol, in a way, of an unresolved war.

A few years ago, they had to disinter someone else from Arlington, and it was anything but a dignified affair. President Clinton's ambassador to Switzerland had claimed right of burial there by virtue of having served in the merchant marine during World War II. He was buried with the usual honors. Shortly thereafter, it turned out that his claim was completely false. The Congress and veterans howled in protest and there followed one of those debates that provide excellent raw material for late-night TV. In due course, he was exhumed and removed to less hallowed ground. I fear this will not help my own campaign to be buried here.

I sat in the shade and watched the Old Guard. They parade back and forth in front of the Unknowns from World War I and II and Korea, 24 hours a day, 365 days a year. It's a tribute to their perfection, rather than disrespectful, to say that they look utterly mechanical, these soldiers, as they pace 21 steps, stop, face the tomb for 21 seconds in honor of a silent 21-gun salute, pivot with a sharp report of metal heel on heel, and walk back, over and over and over. Their training is meticulous, as is their endurance. They wear wool uniforms in summer because only these will hold the crease. By regulation, their belts are size 29 inch. But then if you or I paraded in wool in summer, we'd be down to a 29-inch waist, too.

When I worked at the White House, I would sometimes go and watch official welcoming ceremonies for foreign heads of state on the South Lawn. In July or August, these occasions were just killers for the poor soldiers who had to stand there for two hours or more holding flags and carbines while the prime minister of Uruguay droned on about the historic synergy between our two great countries. Often, they would faint, and the protocol was that they had to be left there on the ground until the ceremony was over. It was surreal. There'd be four or five soldiers lying there facedown on the White House lawn, with cannons firing the salute going on and the band playing the national anthem of Uruguay.

I remember the welcoming ceremony for President Anwar Sadat of Egypt. I was standing not far from him and President Reagan. It was a million degrees that day. Sweat was *pouring* off Sadat—an Egyptian! President Reagan stood there, not a bead on him, every hair in place. It was as if they'd kept him in a freezer overnight. I remember Sadat's baritone voice booming over the loudspeakers, "A-merica, you are a *great* companion." We loved Sadat.

Six weeks later, on October 6, 1981, our phones rang. Sadat was dead, machine-gunned as he reviewed a military parade. I remember after that watching Bush's Secret

Service men keeping pace with him whenever he reviewed foreign troops, one right behind him, another shadowing him on the other side of the troops, eyes like wolves.

I wanted to find Major Audie Murphy, the most decorated soldier of World War II. I walked over to Section 46 but couldn't find him. I walked up and down endless rows of stone. *Died in Fire and Explosions USS Forrestal July 29, 1967 Gulf of Tonkin Vietnam US Navy.* Eighteen men. That conflagration burned for hours and took the lives of a total of 129 men. It was ignited when jet exhaust accidentally ignited the missile on a fighter jet parked on the flight deck. The missile launched into the nearby jet of one Lt. John McCain. McCain later became one of the Vietnam War's noblest heroes when he endured five and a half years of torture and confinement as a prisoner of war. His grandfather was a distinguished naval aviator and staff officer during World War II. His father was a World War II submariner and commander in chief of the U.S. naval forces in Vietnam. They're both buried here.

I kept looking for Audie Murphy. *Died in airplane crash February 1 1966 Antarctica.* Three men. *Died in Vietnam October 8, 1967.* Sixteen men. *In honor of members of the United States Armed Forces who died during an attempt to rescue American hostages held in Iran 25 April 1980. . . .* The thought came to me that before taking office, presidents-elect ought to come to Arlington before their swearing-in and browse these lawns.

It was getting late and there were still more graves to see, so I gave up my search for Audie Murphy. As I was leaving Section 46, I came across a man visiting from Indiana who was also looking for Audie Murphy. *Looking for Audie Murphy* would make a good title, for something.

We both scratched our heads and compared notes and agreed to keep looking. We finally found him. Our mistake had been to look for a bigger marker than the standard issue. But the most decorated soldier of World War II has a regulation headstone. The fellow from Indiana was a military buff. He helped me decode the citations on Major Murphy's stone: Medal of Honor; Distinguished Service Cross, Silver Star with Oak Leaf Cluster; Legion of Merit, Bronze Star of Merit with Oak Leaf Clusters; Purple Heart and Oak Leaf Clusters. It's a good thing his valor stopped there or they would have run out of room. There was a line that Reagan used to quote from James Michener's book about the Korean War, *The Bridges at Toko-Ri:* "Where do we get such men?"

And women. In Section 8 you'll find the grave of Marie Therese Rossi, Major, U.S. Army. Her stone reads:

FIRST FEMALE COMBAT COMMANDER TO FLY INTO BATTLE
OPERATION DESERT STORM.

Below that it says: "In Memory of My Sweet Little Wife, Whose Beauty Could Only Be Outlived by My Love for Her."

I wanted to pay my respects to Joe Louis, the great boxer. I shook his hand once, in of all places, Las Vegas, where he was employed by Caesars Palace casino in that sad capacity of "official greeter," the last rung on the way back down the ladder of fame. But he maintained his dignity intact, even as he glad-handed high rollers who slapped him on the back and called him "Champ" and asked him what he was drinking. His gravestone contains a medallion-shaped bronze relief showing him in fighting pose with gloves and trunks and reads,

> *The Brown Bomber*
> *World Heavyweight Champion 1937–1949*

He wasn't strictly speaking eligible for burial at Arlington, but President Reagan took care of it.

James Tanner, the double-amputee stenographer who took it all down the night of April 14–15, 1865, at the Petersen House, is in Section 2, below the Arlington House. Everyone is here. I wanted to pay my respects to Dashiell Hammett and Medgar Evers, Oliver Wendell Holmes Jr. and General Jimmy Doolittle, but it was getting on, and having spent a memorable night in my youth being chased by Dobermans through a cemetery, I tend toward exactitude in the matter of cemetery closing times.

There are now 260,000 graves at Arlington, giving it roughly half the population of Washington, D.C. They will run out of room in the year 2020, so the requirements for being planted here are getting more and more stringent. It's really not looking very good for me. I'd better make out a codicil to my will with instructions to sneak in my ashes in a brown paper bag.

At the bend of the driveway as it turns toward Arlington House is the grave of General George Crook, who died in 1890. With all respect to the general, this has to be the most politically incorrect grave at Arlington. After his exploits in the Civil War, which were numerous enough, he went on, like his colleague Phil Sheridan, to wiping out Indians. His campaigns in that sorry endeavor are enumerated on his stone: *Rogue River, Pit River, Shastas, Wascoes, Modocs, Piutes, Bannocks, Shoshones, Apaches, Sioux, Cheyenne, Utes, Nez Perces, Apaches.* One side reveals a meticulous bronze bas relief depicting the *Surrender of Apaches Under Geronimo to General Crook in the Sierra Madre Mountains, Mexico 1883.* All the participants are identified: *Geronymo, Chato, Loco, Peaches.* In his straw hat, General Crook looks like he's enjoying a splendid picnic. I'm sure it wasn't.

It was really getting on now, so I walked along the driveway back to the house, past the graves of the soldiers whom Meigs had planted here: *John M. Smith Capt. 110 Regt. Ohio Inf 27 May 1864.* He had the same name as the first white man to set eyes on this hillside, in 1608—Captain John Smith. I read more names as I crunched on gravel. *John Goulding, Lt. 16 NY Cav. 5 July 1865.* He died of his wounds three months after the surrender at Appomattox.

On the steps of the mansion, another guide was gamely shouting out his narration to the never-ending line of high schoolers. As James Michener would say, *Where do we get such kids?*

The guide pointed at the granite slab in front of the mansion, in the shade of an old tree just at the crest of the hill that slopes down toward the Kennedy grave, and beyond to the river, Arlington Memorial Bridge, the Lincoln Memorial, Reflecting Pool, Mall, Washington Monument, and the Capitol Dome.

"That's Pierre L'Enfant," he said. "He DESIGNED WASHINGTON, D.C., and what *HE* was about was *BAD ATTITUDE*. You know the three rules? Courtesy, cooperation, and consideration? These are THREE THINGS that L'Enfant had *NOOOO* concept of. Finally Washington had to FIRE HIM. So there's good attitude and BAD attitude. GOOD attitude will take you a LONG WAY, a lot farther than your brain or feet will get you."

My 1885 edition of *Keim's Illustrated Handbook* notes, "The last days of his life were spent around Washington. He found a home on the farm of Mr. Digges, and died in the summer of 1825, at the advanced age of 70 years. His remains still moulder beneath the sod where the kind hand of charity laid them."

In 1909, the injustice was finally rectified. The sum of one thousand dollars was made available to the commissioners for the District of Columbia "to remove and render accessible to the public the grave of Major Pierre

Charles L'Enfant." According to a contemporary account, the exhumers found "a lonely and unmarked grave more than six feet in length. A graceful, red cedar, drawing its vigorous life from the very earth which enveloped the ashes of the neglected Frenchman, his sole monument for eighty-four years, swaying and whispering with every breeze, carried the inspiration of his genius into never-ending requiem, while its pungent odor served as perpetual incense."

Their digging was interrupted by a thunderstorm. Finally, their spades hit the coffin. "As the party stood with uncovered heads around the excavation," the account continues, "the transfer of the remains of the famous engineer was begun. A cardinal bird, sitting in a near-by tree, sang almost continuously during the work at the grave."

In the Capitol Rotunda, in the building he had perched atop Jenkins Hill, L'Enfant's bones were accorded the great honor of resting in a casket atop the catafalque upon which Lincoln's casket had lain. According to the *Evening Star's* account, at his new gravesite were "many men distinguished in the councils of the nation. Three volleys were fired by troopers of the 15th Cavalry, and a lone bugler played 'Taps' following a prayer by Rev. Father Russell."

And so, on April 28, L'Enfant reached his final resting place, buried on the hill overlooking the city that he and George Washington conjured into existence. Commissioner Macfarland provided the most apt epitaph in his speech in the Rotunda. He said he hoped to see a statue of L'Enfant in a park someday. Of course, no diligent city commissioner would commit himself, even on such a solemn occasion. "But the beauty of the city itself," he added, "increasing with the years, will always be the best remembrancer of his fame." Not such a bad end, after all.

SOURCES AND BIBLIOGRAPHY

Adams, Henry. *Democracy, An American Novel.* New York: Meridian, 1994.

Alexander, John. *Ghosts! Washington Revisited: The Ghostlore of the Nation's Capital.* Atglen, Pa.: Schiffer Publishing, 1998.

Alsop, Joseph W., with Adam Platt. *"I've Seen the Best of It": Memoirs.* New York: W.W. Norton, 1992.

Applewhite, E. J. *Washington Itself: An Informal Guide to the Capital of the United States.* New York: Alfred A. Knopf, 1989.

Bigler, Philip. *In Honored Glory: Arlington National Cemetery, The Final Post,* 3rd edition. Clearwater, Fla.: Vandamere Press, 2001.

Boller, Paul F., Jr. *Presidential Anecdotes.* New York: Oxford University Press, 1981.

———. *Presidential Campaigns.* New York: Oxford University Press, 1984.

Borowski, Tadeusz. *This Way for the Gas, Ladies and Gentlemen.* New York: Penguin Books, 1976.

Bowling, Kenneth R. *Coming into the Country, Essays on Early Washington, D.C.: Commemorating the Bicentennial of the Federal Government's Arrival in 1800.* Washington, D.C.: The Historical Society of Washington, D.C., 2000.

Caemmerer, H. P. *Washington: The National Capital.* Washington, D.C.: U.S. Government Printing Office, 1932.

Carrier, Thomas J. *Images of America—Washington, D.C.: A Historical Walking Tour.* Charleston, S.C.: Arcadia Publishing, 2000.

Sources and Bibliography

Carrier, Thomas J. *Images of America—The White House, The Capitol, and the Supreme Court: Historic Self-Guided Tours.* Charleston, S.C.: Arcadia Publishing, 2000.

Choukas-Bradley, Melanie, and Polly Alexander. *City of Trees: The Complete Field Guide to the Trees of Washington, D.C.* Baltimore: Johns Hopkins University Press, 1987.

Chronicle of the 20th Century. Liberty, Mo.: JL International Publishing, 1992.

Cleveland Park. Washington, D.C.: Moore & Hill, 1904.

Cooper, Frederic Taber. *Rider's Washington: A Guide Book for Travelers.* New York: MacMillan Company, 1924.

Dieterle, Lorraine Jacyno. *Arlington National Cemetery: A Nation's Story Carved in Stone.* San Francisco: Pomegranate, 2001.

Donald, David Herbert. *Lincoln.* New York: Simon & Schuster, 1995.

Ehrlichman, John. *Witness to Power.* Simon and Schuster, 1982.

Executive Office of the President, Office of Administration. *The Old Executive Office Building: A Victorian Masterpiece.* Washington, D.C.: U.S. Government Printing Office, 1984.

Finamore, Frank J. *Washington, D.C. Trivia Fact Book.* New York: Gramercy Books, 2001.

Fogle, Jeanne. *Proximity to Power: Neighbors to the Presidents Near Lafayette Square.* Washington, D.C.: A Tour de Force Publication, 1999.

Foote, Shelby. *The Civil War: A Narrative—Fort Sumter to Perryville* (Vol. 1). New York: Vintage, 1986.

———. *The Civil War: A Narrative—Fredericksburg to Meridian* (Vol. 2). New York: Vintage, 1986.

———. *The Civil War: A Narrative—Red River to Appomattox* (Vol. 3). New York: Vintage, 1986.

Ford, Elise Hartman. *Frommer's Memorable Walks in Washington, D.C.*, 3rd edition. New York: MacMillan Travel USA, 1999.

———. *Frommer's Washington, D.C. 2002.* New York: Hungry Minds, 2002.

Froncek, Thomas, ed. *The City of Washington: An Illustrated History, by the Junior League of Washington.* New York: Alfred A. Knopf, 1981.

Garrison, Webb. *A Treasury of White House Tales.* Nashville, Tenn.: Rutledge Hill Press, 1996.

Green, Constance McLaughlin. *Washington: Village and Capital, 1800–1878.* Princeton, N.J.: Princeton University Press, 1962.

Harger, Laura. *Washington, D.C.* Oakland, Calif.: Lonely Planet, 2001.

"Honor to L'Enfant Tardy but Sincere." *The Evening Star* (Washington, D.C.), April 28, 1909: Section 1, p. 1.

Höss, Rudolf, Pery Broad, and Johann Paul Kremer. *KL Auschwitz Seen by the SS.* Oświęcim, Poland: Auschwitz-Birkenau State Museum, 1998.

Keim, DeB. Randolph. *Keim's Illustrated Hand-book of Washington and Its Environs.* Washington, D.C., 1885.

Keneally, Thomas. *American Scoundrel: The Life of the Notorious Civil War General Dan Sickles.* New York: Nan A. Talese/Doubleday, 2002.

Kelly, Charles Suddarth. *Washington, D.C., Then and Now: 69 Sites Photographed in the Past and Present.* New York: Dover Publications, 1984.

Lee, Richard M. *Mr. Lincoln's City: An Illustrated Guide to the Civil War Sites of Washington.* McLean, Va.: EPM Publications, 1981.

Levey, Bob, and Jane Freundel Levey. *Washington Album: A Pictoral History of the Nation's Capital.* Washington, D.C.: Washington Post Books, 2000.

Lopes, Sal, et al. *The Wall: Images and Offerings from the Vietnam Veterans Memorial.* New York: Collins Publishers, 1987.

Mann-Kenney, Louise. *Rosedale: The Eighteenth Century Country Estate of General Uriah Forrest, Cleveland Park, Washington, D.C.* Washington, D.C.: Youth for Understanding International Exchange/Queene Ferry Coonley Foundation/Uriah Forrest Descendants, 1989.

McKay, Kathryn. *Around Washington, D.C. with Kids.* New York: Fodor's Travel Publications, 2000.

McPherson, James M., ed. *"To the Best of My Ability": The American Presidents.* New York: Dorling Kindersley, 2001.

Melder, Keith. *City of Magnificent Intentions: A History of Washington, District of Columbia,* 2nd ed. Washington, D.C.: Intac, 1997.

Meredith, Roy. *The World of Mathew Brady: Portraits of the Civil War Period.* New York: Bonanza Books, 1976.

Morgan, James Dudley. "The Reinterment of Major Pierre Charles L'Enfant." Records of the Columbia Historical Society, Washington, D.C., 1910: Vol. 13, pp. 119–205.

Morris, Edmund. *Theodore Rex*. New York: Random House, 2001.

Morris, Jan. *Destinations: Essays from Rolling Stone.* New York: Oxford University Press/Rolling Stone, 1982.

National Park Service. *Lincoln Memorial: A Guide to the Lincoln Memorial, District of Columbia*. Washington, D.C.: U.S. Department of the Interior, 1986.

Nilsson, Dex. *The Names of Washington, D.C.* Rockville, Md.: Twinbrook Communications, 2000.

Oxford One-Volume Illustrated Encyclopedia. New York: Oxford University Press, 1997.

Padover, Saul K., ed. *Jefferson and the National Capital*. Washington, D.C.: U.S. Government Printing Office, 1946.

Pearson, Hesketh. *Oscar Wilde: His Life and Wit*. New York: Harper & Brothers, 1946.

Penczer, Peter R. *Washington D.C. Past & Present*. Arlington, Va.: Oneonta Press, 1998.

Pitch, Anthony S. *Exclusively Presidential Trivia*. Potomac, Md.: Mino Publications, 2001.

———. *Exclusively Washington Trivia*. Potomac, Md.: Mino Publications, 2001.

———. *A Walk in the Past: Georgetown*. Potomac, Md.: Mino Publications, 1999.

Proctor, John Clagett. "L'Enfant Vision of Future Was Forecast of Beauty of Capital." *The Sunday Star* (Washington, D.C.), March 3, 1929: Part 7.

Rash, Bryson B. *Footnote Washington: Tracking the Engaging, Humorous and Surprising Bypaths of Capital History*. McLean, Va.: EPM Publications, 1981.

Reed, Robert. *Old Washington D.C. in Early Photographs, 1846–1932*. New York: Dover Publications, 1980.

Reynolds, Charles B. *Washington: The Nation's Capital*. New York: Foster & Reynolds, 1912.

Schafer, Edith Nalle. *Literary Circles of Washington*. Washington, D.C.: Starrhill Press, 1993.

Scott, Pamela. "L'Enfant's Washington Described: The City in the Public Press, 1791–1795." *Washington History: Magazine of the*

Historical Society of Washington, D.C., Spring/Summer 1991: Vol. 3, No. 1, pp. 96–111.

Slayden, Ellen Maury. *Washington Wife: Journal of Ellen Maury Slayden from 1897–1919.* New York: Harper & Row, 1963.

Stapen, Candyce H. *Washington, D.C. Blue Guide.* New York: W.W. Norton, 2000.

Thompson, John. *National Geographic Traveler: Washington, D.C.* Washington, D.C.: National Geographic Society, 2002.

Trager, James. *The People's Chronology: A Year-by-Year Record of Human Events from Prehistory to the Present.* New York: Henry Holt, 1992.

Truett, Randall Bond, ed. *Washington, D.C.: A Guide to the Nation's Capital, New Revised Edition.* New York: Hastings House, 1968.

Twain, Mark, and Charles Dudley Warner. *The Gilded Age.* New York: Oxford University Press, 1996.

Wallechinsky, David, and Irving Wallace. *The People's Almanac.* Garden City, N.Y.: Doubleday & Company, 1975.

Washington Merry-Go-Round. New York: Horace Liveright, 1931.

Weeks, Christopher. *AIA Guide to the Architecture of Washington D.C.*, 3rd ed. Baltimore: Johns Hopkins University Press, 1994.

White House Historical Association. *The White House: An Historic Guide.* Washington, D.C.: National Geographic Society, 1979.

Whitman, William B. *Washington, D.C.: Off the Beaten Path.* Guilford, Conn.: Globe Pequot Press, 2001.

Whitney, David C. *The American Presidents,* 4th edition. Garden City, N.Y.: Doubleday & Company, 1978.

Wilson, Vincent, Jr., ed. *The Book of Great American Documents.* Brookeville, Md.: American History Research Associates, 1998.

Wilson, Vincent, Jr. *The Book of the Presidents.* Brookeville, Md.: American History Research Associates, 2001.

Winik, Jay. *April 1865: The Month That Saved America.* New York: HarperCollins, 2001.

Young, Don, and Marjorie Young. *Walking Places in Washington, D.C.* Asheville, N.C.: Out There Press, 2001.

Acknowledgments

I'M GRATEFUL TO the authors of the many books cited in here who got there first. I'm indebted to Matthew Reed Baker for pointing out my many factual errors while there was still time to correct them, and for his skilled exhumations amid the historical catacombs. Doug Pepper of Crown wanted the book, Amanda Urban sold it to him. Thanks again to Patrick Cooke for the title. Thanks also to Jerome Cramer for pointing out how dreadful the original Capitol chapter was and for helping me land that trophy trout in Ireland. Thank you, Michelle Laxalt and Pete Teeley, for bringing me to D.C. in the first place. Thank you, Lucy, WFB, Jr., and PTB for the enthusiasm, and special thanks to the Faithful Hound Jake, who demanded to be let out every time I was really cooking.

About the Author

CHRISTOPHER BUCKLEY moved to Washington, D.C., in 1981, intending to remain there for one year. He is still there.

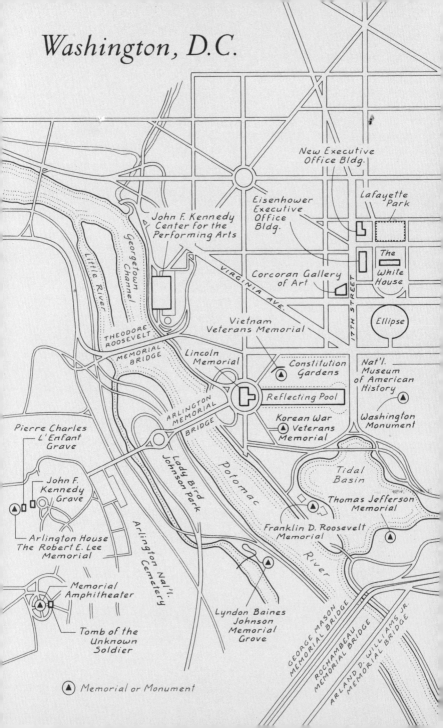

Washington, D.C.

New Executive
Office Bldg.

Lafayette
Park

Eisenhower
Executive
Office
Bldg.

The
White
House

John F. Kennedy
Center for the
Performing Arts

Corcoran Gallery
of Art

Georgetown Channel

Little River

VIRGINIA AVE.

17TH STREET

Ellipse

THEODORE
ROOSEVELT

Vietnam
Veterans Memorial

MEMORIAL
BRIDGE

Lincoln
Memorial

Constitution
Gardens

Nat'l.
Museum
of American
History

Reflecting Pool

Washington
Monument

ARLINGTON
MEMORIAL
BRIDGE

Korean War
Veterans
Memorial

Pierre Charles
L'Enfant
Grave

Lady Bird
Johnson Park

Potomac

Tidal
Basin

John F.
Kennedy
Grave

Thomas Jefferson
Memorial

Arlington Nat'l. Cemetery

Franklin D. Roosevelt
Memorial

Arlington House
The Robert E. Lee
Memorial

River

Memorial
Amphitheater

Tomb of the
Unknown
Soldier

Lyndon Baines
Johnson
Memorial
Grove

GEORGE MASON MEMORIAL BRIDGE

ROCHAMBEAU MEMORIAL BRIDGE

ARLAND D. WILLIAMS JR. MEMORIAL BRIDGE

▲ Memorial or Monument